MOVING THE MASSES

PILLARS OF PROPHETIC PREACHING

REGINALD WADE WILLIAMS, JR.

KATARA WASHINGTON PATTON, EDITOR

FOREWORD BY JOHN W. KINNEY
AFTERWORD BY ALISON GISE-JOHNSON
EPILOGUE BY MATTHEW WILLIAMS

JUDSON PRESS
PUBLISHERS SINCE 1824
VALLEY FORGE, PA

Judson Press has made every effort to trace the ownership of all quotes. In the event of a question arising from the use of a quote, we regret any error made and will be pleased to make the necessary correction in future printings and editions of this book.

Bible quotations in this volume are from the New Revised Standard Version of the Bible, copyright © 1989 by the Division of Christian Education of the National Council of the Churches of Christ in the United States of America. Used by permission. All rights reserved.

Interior design by Crystal Devine.
Cover design by Anthony Aranha.

Library of Congress Cataloging-in-Publication Data

Names: Williams, Reginald W., Jr., author.
Title: Moving the masses : Pillars of prophetic preaching / Reginald W Williams, Jr. ; foreword by John Kinney ; afterword by Alison Gise-Johnson.
Description: Valley Forge, PA : Judson Press, 2021. | Includes bibliographical references and index.
Identifiers: LCCN 2021011257 (print) | LCCN 2021011258 (ebook) | ISBN 9780817018252 (trade paperback) | ISBN 9780817082284 (epub)
Subjects: LCSH: Preaching. | Prophecy--Christianity.
Classification: LCC BV4221 .W55 2021 (print) | LCC BV4221 (ebook) | DDC 251--dc23
LC record available at https://lccn.loc.gov/2021011257
LC ebook record available at https://lccn.loc.gov/2021011258

Printed in the U.S.A.

First printing, 2021.

CONTENTS

APPENDIX

ACKNOWLEDGMENTS

With deep reflection, I have come to realize that this book has been in the making for some time. Part of this book began to take shape during my masters and doctoral studies at the Samuel DeWitt Proctor School of Theology at Virginia Union. With professors who also were practitioners, my theological education was liberating and life changing. Still other parts of the book come from connecting the dots in my own story. My parents met at an Operation Breadbasket hunger campaign and were both intricately involved in the Black church and Black freedom struggle. Our family's membership at Trinity United Church of Christ in Chicago, under the pastorate of Rev. Dr. Jeremiah A. Wright, Jr., gave us spiritual grounding which affirmed our authenticity as African people, and moved us to do justice, love mercy, and walk humbly with our God. The combination and connection of my journey, with my love of preaching, and concern for justice has made this a labor of love, and the work my soul must have, in the words of the beloved late Dr. Katie G. Canon. With Sankofa sensibilities, and an understanding of Ubuntu, I am aware that there are many to which I owe a great debt of thanksgiving.

I am aware that I am but a link in a chain of a tradition of a people. I therefore must take time to honor ancestors, some whose names I will never know, for their deposits in what is now the soil of my soul. With deep gratitude, I am grateful for the life, love, and legacy of venerable ancestors Dr. Katie Geneva Canon and Dr. Miles Jerome Jones whose care and concern in the classroom nudged and nurtured me and countless others academically.

I am grateful to my Virginia Union Family at the Samuel DeWitt Proctor School of Theology. Dr. Alison Gise Johnson and Dr. John Kinney empowered me to chew, challenge, and confront theological concepts that served to stretch and strengthen my work and walk. Dr. Patricia Gould Champ and Dr. Jessica Young Brown, I am grateful for your shepherding through the doctoral process and challenging me to go deeper and expand my thinking. To my classmates both in the MDiv and DMin programs, I'm grateful for your presence and push. My classmates from the entering class of 1999, the Doctoral Cohort Nexus, and the "Four Horsemen" deserve mention.

Thank you, Pastor Rev. Dr. Jeremiah A. Wright, Jr., for your meaningful model of cultural integrity through your preaching and teaching. Sitting in your classroom every Sunday at 400 W. 95th Street and watching you move in ministry is a privilege. Sitting at your feet as an "intercessee" and lifetime student is an honor.

To the family of faith at First Baptist Church of University Park, where I am privileged to partner as pastor, I am grateful for your warm, winsome, and welcoming spirit as we continue to live the love of Christ in community through worship, witness, and works.

I am grateful to the faculty, staff, and students who have studied the meaning, method, and movements as offered in this book and encouraged me to put them into print. I'm grateful to the Samuel DeWitt Proctor School of Theology at Virginia Union, Chicago Theological

Seminary, and McCormick Theological Seminary for trusting me with the responsibility of teaching. I'm grateful for the students in the aforementioned institutions and workshop participants elsewhere, who have studied and offered suggestions as they engaged the particulars around prophetic preaching's meaning and method.

Special mention must be made of Carla Jackson, Kimberly Clark, Steven G. Blunt, William Marcus Small & Eugene Gibson (Pack), the horsemen: Eric Jason Gill, George Joseph Mitchell and Joshua Mitchell, Melva Sampson, Stacey Edwards-Dunn, Nathan Quick, James Jackson, Gregory Howard, Paul Flowers, Earle Fisher, Hodari Williams, Stephanie Crumpton, Frederick D. Haynes III, Kenyatta Gilbert, Mark Lomax, Stephanie Buckhanon Crowder, Terance McNeil, O'Neal Larkin, Junious Brown, David Wilson, Nathaniel Moultrie, Sheleta Fomby, Ebony Only, Amber Coates, Justin Hamler, James Bryson, Eddie Williams III, Itihare Touré, Father Michael Pfleger, Leslie Dawn Calahan, Veronica Johnson, David Watkins, III, Danielle Ayers, Heber Brown, III., Tyrone Nelson, D. Mitchell Ford, Romal Tune, Rudy & Juanita Rasmus, Warren Mitchell, KeaJuanis Malena, Byron Harris, Charles Barnes, Joel Johnson, Nomarchs of the Nu Umoja, Iva Caruthers, Jerome Ross, Kristal Madgett, Tracey Webster, Ivey Matute, Janet Wright-Moore, Jeri Wright, Dana Garner, Leslie Anderson Rutland. Through your ministry, conversations, reflections, prayers, challenging, or confronting, you have encouraged me in some way that has contributed to the birth of this book. I am aware that I may have missed some names. However, let me acknowledge anyone who has planted seeds, given time, reflection, input, or any effort. Thank you!

Special thanks to the staff at Judson. Rebecca Irwin-Diehl, thank you for your service and prayers over the years. Gale Tull, Linda Johnson-LeBlanc, Lisa Blair, and Cheryl Price, thank you for your patience and professionalism. Katara Washington Patton, thank you once again for your keen eye and attention to detail in the editing process.

To my father, Dr. Reginald Williams, Sr., I am humbled to be named after you. You embody all that is the best of Black manhood and fatherhood. To Mommy, thank you for walking with me as a great and mighty ancestor! Your unconditional love, which extends beyond death, continues to remind me each and every day to be your "prince." To Matthew and Joy, I love you and am grateful for your love and our connection! What is understood need not be expressed. We won.

This book is dedicated to my Princesses, Nia Mar'Celle (Purpose) and Laila Imani (Princess)! I pray that you always walk to the beat of the sound of the authentic in you! You are enough! Thank you for choosing me, teaching me, and loving me. I pray that the messages and movements that come from this book help change the world into one that affirms your authenticity. Nia, when you were born, "A Love Supreme" by John Coltrane was playing in the birthing room. Laila, when you were born, "As" by Stevie Wonder was playing in the birthing room. Both of these songs are still inadequate to express the unconditional eternal love I have for you! I love you always with the most supreme love I can offer!

Be Well! Be Authentic! Be!
Reginald Wade Williams, Jr.
January 2021

FOREWORD

Soon after launching my teaching career, I was walking across the campus of Virginia Union University and conversing with Dr. Miles Jerome Jones. As we strolled, we encountered Dr. John Malcus Ellison engaging a group of students. Dr. Ellison was the first African American president of the University, and a thoughtful scholar, gifted writer, able administrator, and distinctive homiletician who had a deep concern for the quality of pulpit oration. Upon seeing Dr. Ellison, Miles Jones put his hand on my shoulder, arresting my steps, and remarked, "I hope those students recognize they are privileged to be in the presence of greatness."

As I reflect on what Dr. Jones said, and I think about the gifts of mind, person, and Spirit that he expressed in his own life and teachings, I would argue that his comment about Dr. Ellison can also be appropriately applied to him. In *Moving the Masses: Pillars of Prophetic Preaching*, Dr. Reginald Williams clearly indicates that he is one of those students who recognizes that, in the pronouncements, practices, and person of Dr. Miles Jones, we witnessed a unique transformative presence. In this work, Dr. Williams illuminates the preaching methodology taught by Dr. Jones in a fashion that does not absolutize a singular method as the medium for truth.

Effective preaching can never be reduced to the framework for the discourse, but every effective sermon indicates some form of an operative constructive framework. There are diverse methods of preaching that can be appropriated and applied, and the "value" of each can be interpreted, modeled, and compared. Dr. Williams introduces us to multiple scholars and practitioners and their understandings of the definition, nature, task, and method of preaching. He also examines and explores Dr. Jones's method of correlation in preaching at length. The correlational method is lifted as an approach supporting prophetic preaching because it brings together world and Word, trouble and truth, situation and sacred, condition of existence, and charismatic encounter. The method carries us through a problematic reality—to a prophetic response, a promised resolution, and a people rejoicing.

Nevertheless, while the method of correlation is explicated thoroughly, Dr. Williams also argues that the foundation for Dr. Jones's method is authenticity. Without authenticity, the sound emerging from any method rings hollow. In truth, authenticity stretches and even obliterates any mechanical barrier that assigns sovereignty to a method. Echoing Howard Thurman and Miles Jones, Dr. Williams reminds us that we must hear and follow the "sound of the genuine." Failure to center in the genuine places our witness and our word at the end of strings pulled by something or somebody else. Preaching that emanates from the genuine permits us to embody the truth and use words only when necessary.

Effective preaching conveys Spirit, structure, substance, and self. The Spirit invites structure and substance but compels the complete offering of the self. When the self is alienated from the preaching moment, it becomes a detached performance rather than the practice of the Presence. Authenticity allows for integrity, vulnerability, genuine faith, and embodied proclamation where the Word becomes flesh. In the absence of the genuine, we can preach and write about the prophetic and the liberative, while our "being" emits a style and modality that remains oppressive. We can easily slip into a form of disassociated dualism where the words of our mouths and the essences of our presence communicate a dissonance that suggests we are still serving the concepts and categories that counter the prophetic. In other words, while Godly words pass through our lips, a heart far from God is revealed.

Walking in authenticity, Miles Jones eschewed being defined, assessed, or explained by other people's philosophical and interpretive categories. He lamented that so much of black scholarship was being coerced and controlled by a process that legitimated thinking through conformance to somebody else's thinking. He suggested, in this process, that the genius of black minding was missed and minimized because the person in the footnote controlled the discourse and the meaning. To Dr. Jones, it was important to, in his words, "Let my being and my life speak for me."

Dr. Jones not only taught powerful and meaningful concepts, but he also dared to "be" what he taught and preached. It has been said that the real depth in preaching is not in what the preacher preaches but rather in what the people become. Affirming this suggestion, I join Dr. Williams in celebrating the transformative life and ministry of Dr. Miles Jerome Jones because all who have been touched and taught by him have become better. Himself truly touched and taught, Reggie Williams invites us to celebrate a powerful teacher and model, embrace his teachings, and be prophetic preachers in proclamation and praxis.

If we are authentic preachers, we can help the world become a better place and all of us become a better people. We can be agents in fulfilling the preaching moment when justice flows like a river, and all God's children can sing "Free at Last."

John W. Kinney
Professor of Theology
Samuel DeWitt Procter School of Theology
Virginia Union University

INTRODUCTION

In 1980, at the Spelman College baccalaureate service, Howard Thurman addressed the graduates with these words.

> There is something in every one of you that waits, listens for the genuine in yourself—and if you cannot hear it, you will never find whatever it is for which you are searching and if you hear it and then do not follow it, it was better that you had never been born. You are the only you that has ever lived; your idiom is the only idiom of its kind . . . , and if you cannot hear the sound of the genuine in you, you will all of your life spend your days on the ends of strings that somebody else pulls.[1]

In a world where so many are enticed to be that which they are not, Thurman's admonishment to aim for authenticity is just as needed today as the day he spoke to the 1980 graduates at Spelman College. Thurman encourages us to dig deep and listen for the sound of the genuine in ourselves so that our sounds may join the chorus of other genuine sounds in the family of humanity. In the same speech, Thurman also states that *"there is something that waits and listens for the sound of the genuine in other people."*[2] The lesson that leaps from his lips is that one cannot appreciate the sound of the genuine in others until they have learned to identify and own the sound of the genuine in themselves. This is not an invitation to individuality and rugged individualism as affirmed by the American civil religion of "Americanity." Rather, this is a prophetic push to delve into one's own authenticity in order to genuinely connect with the larger human family through community. This is Ubuntu:[3] I am because we are, and because we are, therefore I am.

You hold in your hand a book that pushes those who practice and perform the craft of prophetic preaching to give attention and intention to ensuring that prophetic preaching emanates from the sound of the genuine in you! That is, this book attempts to tie a common thread from the authenticity of the inner regions of the preacher to a method used to preach prophetically, which prayerfully pushes people toward movement in the world. Three pillars—method, meaning, and movement—are offered to support, strengthen, and structure the practice of prophetic preaching.

WHAT IS PROPHETIC PREACHING?

Prophetic preaching is proclamation born from the internal reckoning of one's soul and social location in the context of community, resulting in the announcement of God-desired alternatives to systems and ways of being affecting God's creation. Prophetic preaching calls us to commit to such God-desired alternatives with countercultural consciousness, courage, and care.

This sacred discourse does not begin with the performance of the preaching moment, but rather within the inner regions of the preacher. These inner regions are connected to life experiences, thoughts, mental models, and even ancestors whose names we will never know. These inner regions are the stories that make us who we are. The three pillars in this book offer meaning and method in a manner that prayerfully encourages movement in and for the masses. The current social climate, in the midst of the movement for Black lives, reveals that we have no time for preaching that is only concerned with personal piety, while not addressing the plunder, poverty, practices, and policies to which the masses of people are subjected. We have no time for preaching a "salvation" that reflects the white western evangelical hijacking and co-optation of the term, for personal means only, while masses of people suffer. In other words, such a "salvation" will suggest that your soul be saved for the afterlife, but not care about saving of your life in the here-and-now. Such a "salvation" will preach powerfully about your new home in glory, while not caring about the homeless on earth. Such a "salvation" will declare that everyone will have a new robe and new shoes in glory, while allowing for people here on earth to remain naked and shoeless. Such a "salvation" will sing about when we all get to heaven, while not saving black and brown bodies worldwide from the policies and practices emboldened by white supremacy, racism, sexism, patriarchy, gender-based violence, homophobia, transphobia, and other evil expressions of domination which many times are supported or permitted by the white evangelical church.

Such an appropriation of the term salvation has been injected into the psyche of the masses, while infecting the same with an interpretation that seduces many into enduring suffering now while waiting for the great by-and-by. This appropriation is not salvation at all, but rather a seduction. It is seducing people to become agreeable and complicit with their own suffering and oppression, while waiting to die and experience that great getting up morning. Such seduction is akin to what was offered in slave religion as a control mechanism. All the while, the same ones who injected and infected those with such theological toxicity, ground themselves in a hierarchical supremacist ideology that masks itself as Christian theology. Such an approach attempts to preserve their privilege, power, and position, while justifying the wholesale denigration and dehumanization of the vulnerable people of the earth.

In most of the Bible, salvation is spoken of not only as a need for security in the afterlife, but also as a need to be saved and rescued from clear, current, present danger. Prophetic preaching must not only advocate for shoes in glory, but also call for policies and practices for people with no shoes on earth. Prophetic preaching must not only sermonize on the beauty of sitting at the welcome table on the other side, but also assertively advocate for a table where all are welcomed with radical hospitality on this side, regardless of race, gender, creed, orientation, or identification. This is the message that must be preached for the masses who too often find themselves welcomed to the table only when they are items on the menu.

Prophetic preaching demands of the preacher the work of intense theological reflection so as not to employ theologies of oppression masked as an effort to support liberation. A serious, courageous calling forth of theological thinkers not afraid to confront, challenge, and even dismiss theological approaches deemed "untouchable" is necessary in order to not only revive preaching but also ensure that preaching and church are relevant. Challenging these deeply held, traditional theological stances may appear heretical, but it can actually lead to healing. When one looks at the historical foundations from which some of these approaches come, it is clear that the aim in espousing such approaches is control, subjugation, and oppression. If prophetic preaching is to be real, relevant, and revolutionary, there must be a refusal to herald oppressive theologies while claiming to aspire to an alternate reality of liberation and freedom.

Prophetic preaching must give voice to matters born from prophetic analysis, articulation, and movement to action. This type of prophetic preaching, however, does not begin with social analysis, but rather with self-introspection. Beginning with self-introspection is a critical practice alongside social analysis. I argue that it is important to begin with self-introspection, lest any preacher or person be guilty of not exercising or endeavoring to exercise the very justice they proclaim ought to be seen in society. As an example, it is disingenuous for one to advocate for a living wage for workers, while not paying their workers a living wage. It is less than honest to advocate against discrimination, while choosing who and what you will discriminate against.

This is an ethical exercise that calls on us to always engage in internal and external critique simultaneously, in order that our proclamation be seasoned with integrity. We must not be guilty of proclaiming justice in the public square while practicing injustice in private. Let us begin from within and proclaim from a place of integrity.

This book aims to serve not only as a substantive contribution to the craft of prophetic preaching in our current day, but also as a Sankofa (looking back while moving forward) submission for those who continue the craft long after our days here are done.

There are a number of authors who have tackled the matter of prophetic preaching with integrity and

authenticity. Leonora Tubbs Tisdale, in her book *Prophetic Preaching*,[4] exposes us to the ingredients and
shows us how they can come together to create a prophetic sermon from a pastoral approach. James Henry
Harris, in *Preaching Liberation*, argues that preaching
liberation, or prophetic preaching, can personally trans-
forms one's own life and publicly transform systems that
"often appear to absorb and nullify individual efforts."[5]
In *The Heart of Black Preaching*,[6] Cleophus LaRue
explores the art of Black preaching—identifying social
justice preaching, in particular, as one of the key pillars in what he calls the "Domains of Experience" and
considering it a form of Black preaching that is essential
to a preaching calendar.

In *Exodus Preaching: Crafting Sermons about Justice and Hope*,[7] Kenyatta Gilbert offers a practical resource that empowers practitioners to craft sermons of
justice and hope through four characteristic markers of
African American prophetic preaching—or, as he terms
it, exodus preaching. Marvin McMickle has written
extensively about prophetic preaching. Particularly, in
Where Have All the Prophets Gone,[8] he nobly reclaims
prophetic preaching from those who would manipulate
it for their own purposes and privileges.

Tisdale, Harris, LaRue, Gilbert, and McMickle,
throughout their texts, help us to see many of the ingredients in the recipe for prophetic preaching. While
all of these are great and critical resources, *Moving the
Masses: Pillars of Prophetic Preaching* differs in its scope
and aim. This book incorporates the inner work of the
preacher and lays out a corresponding method to engage
in prophetic preaching wherein "deep calls unto deep."[9]
Plenty of work has been done on prophetic preaching
as it relates to the mandate for social justice. Much

less work has been done on the connection of personal storying to prophetic preaching, and consequently, the movement of people to prophetically transform society.

Therefore, *Moving the Masses* calls us to consider the craft of prophetic preaching along with a corresponding method for study and practice. Additionally, this book explores the authenticity of the preacher as a basis for prophetic preaching. The corresponding method comes courtesy of the teachings of the late Rev. Dr. Miles Jerome Jones at the Samuel DeWitt Proctor School of Theology at Virginia Union University. Dr. Jones was professor of preaching and worship there, and I and countless other men and women enjoyed the privilege of sitting at his feet as students. His presence and professorial skills ushered many a student into the unknown academic abyss of seminary as a strong and steadying guide. From the first class of seminary, he emphasized the importance of authenticity upon each student. "God knows who God called," he would say. Such a perspective helped calm the raging waters when the question was asked: "Do I belong in seminary?"

I will offer other reflections of Dr. Jones in the introduction to Part 2 of this book, as such reflection is beneficial to understanding the method he taught. As a good student, I have added and amended a few method components that I will also offer. After I taught this method in numerous classes and workshops, students and practitioners encouraged me to put the method in print. For their push, I am grateful. This book is for students in seminaries, ministry leaders and practitioners, those in formal or informal learning environments, and anyone who is interested in prophetic preaching. However, this book is not limited to students only. Others may find great help in sections dealing with authenticity, storying, and other aspects of the book that invite them into deeper levels of self-discovery.

It should be noted that prophetic preaching is only one type of preaching. There are a host of other areas of preaching that demand sermonic attention in order to ground and grace God's people with "A Word from the Lord." Martha Simmons's *Doing the Deed*[10] is another great foundational book on the crafting of a good sermon. Frank Thomas, the pastor emeritus of the Mississippi Boulevard Christian Church in Memphis and the curator of the only PhD program centered on African American preaching, boasts a bibliography ranging from *They Like to Never Quit Praisin' God*[11] to *How to Preach a Dangerous Sermon.*[12] Teresa Fry Brown's *Weary Throats and New Songs*[13] centers the experience of women in preaching through the examination of Black women's preparation, content, delivery, and identity. In comparison, this work is intentional about looking at the area of prophetic preaching with an emphasis on the linkage of the internal life of the preacher to a method of sermon construction that hopefully engages the people for movement.

Each part of this book will examine a pillar of prophetic preaching. Part 1 will address the **MEANING** of prophetic preaching. Chapter 1 will expound on the definition offered, considers other practitioners' definitions, and examines what prophetic preaching is and what it is not. Chapter 2 will also uncover and discover approaches to prophetic preaching that will help the preacher pour from an authentic center in their prophetic preaching. Chapter 3 will provide a working definition of a sermon and describe the definitive content of the same. Part 2 of this book will examine a **METHOD** of prophetic preaching. Chapter by chapter, we will go through the corresponding method that links the authenticity of the preacher to the sermon presented. This is the correlation method taught by Dr. Jones. Part 3 will examine **MOVEMENT** as the third pillar of prophetic preaching. There, we will address the hopes of the prophetic preacher beyond meaning and method, toward "moving the masses."

This is not a book that provides a formula on how to preach a sermon dealing with social justice issues simply because it's popular to do so given the current condition of the country and the world. Rather, this book is meant to usher the reader into an experience and journey that is both educational and transformative. For the practitioner, pupil, professor, or any person who is ready to mine the inner regions in order to deepen their self-discovery, and thereby deepen their preaching to others so that deep calls unto deep, I invite you into the journey to move the masses. Let's get to work!

NOTES

1. Howard Thurman, "The Sound of the Genuine in You." Spelman Baccalaureate Address 1980. Published by Indianapolis University Crossings Project, http://eip.uindy.edu/crossings/publications/reflection4.pdf, accessed September 22, 2016.

2. Ibid.

3. The word Ubuntu is Zulu in origin.

4. Leonora Tubbs Tisdale, *Prophetic Preaching: A Pastoral Approach* (Louisville, KY: Westminster John Knox, 2010.), Kindle Edition.

5. James H. Harris, *Preaching Liberation* (Minneapolis: Fortress Press, 1995).

6. Cleophus LaRue, *The Heart of Black Preaching* (Louisville, KY: Westminster John Knox, 2000).

7. Kenyatta R. Gilbert, *Exodus Preaching: Crafting Sermons about Justice and Hope* (Nashville: Abingdon Press, 2018).

8. Marvin A. McMickle, *Where Have All the Prophets Gone?: Reclaiming Prophetic Preaching in America* (Cleveland: Pilgrim Press, 2019).

9. This is a reference to Psalm 42:7.

10. Martha Simmons, *Doing the Deed* (Atlanta: The African American Pulpit, 2012).

11. Frank Thomas, *They Like to Never Quit Praisin' God: The Role of Celebration in Preaching* (Cleveland: Pilgrim Press, 2013).

12. Frank Thomas, *How to Preach a Dangerous Sermon* (Nashville: Abingdon Press, 2018).

13. Teresa L. Fry Brown, *Weary Throats and New Songs* (Nashville: Abingdon Press, 2003).

MEANING

CHAPTER 1

WHAT IS PROPHETIC PREACHING?

How shall they hear without a preacher?
—ROMANS 10:14

PROPHETIC PREACHING

While attending a workshop in Memphis, Tennessee, in 2015, a fire alarm went off, causing quite a bit of confusion at the conference. In order to ensure the safety and security of the conferees, the officials at the hotel instructed us to leave the building until further notice. As conferees exited the building, our conversation was filled with a common theme of concern and confusion, as we waited and wondered when we would be allowed back into the center to continue the conference. Some conversation centered on what could have caused the alarm—was it a drill or was there some real danger? While none of us could see any fire, nor smell any smoke, the alarm arrested our attention to advise us through a striking and startling sound that something was wrong. It also caused us to quickly follow instructions and evacuate the building. Because it was connected to a central surveillance system, the same alarm that arrested our attention was also alerting the proper authorities that intervention was needed to restore a sense of safety and security. Additionally, the same alarm, while arresting our attention, also offered us the expectation that assistance and intervention was on the way.

Prophetic preaching serves in a similar manner, as an alarm, if you will. In order to operate effectively, the prophetic preacher must be connected to the central surveillance system through which all of us live, move, and have our being. The intention and attention given to the inner life of the preacher is of primary importance for prime effectiveness. Prayer, meditation, solitude, and storying (for which I argue later in the book) are just a few of the internal practices that serve to fill and sustain the wells from which the prophetic preacher will pour into those the preacher serves. Staying connected to the central surveillance system is important so the alarm sounded by the preacher is not a false or phony alarm, but an alarm that earnestly and honestly arrests the attention of the masses and provides them with assurance that help is on the way. In other words, the alarm offers hope that although the present reality may cause confusion, chaos, and conflict, there is help on the way from the proper authorities to bring forth an alternative reality of restoration, reformation, and rejuvenation from the current social order.

To begin to understand prophetic preaching's role, we must define just what this form of preaching is to alleviate confusion surrounding the label. Understandably, the term "prophetic" alone is enough to spark debates, conversations, and inquiries in many church and religious circles, especially given historical as well as contemporary usage of the word. Some have taken prophetic preaching to mean those who are especially gifted by God to be fortune-tellers and predictors of future events and end times. More often than not, these are based on notions of biblical literalism, and traditionalism, especially as it relates to apocalyptic literature. According to Obery Hendricks in his critical and classic book, *The Politics of Jesus*,[1] "Today, prophecy is thought to be solely synonymous with foretelling the future. . . . The purpose of prophecy seems to be to offer predictions about love, money, career promotions, and other personal concerns."[2] They use modern-day views of those who send messages about the future as a tool of manipulation for money, and material gain. (Think the soothsayer or the ominous one with cards who can tell you when you will receive fortune or misfortune.) These only bear a small semblance of relatedness to the biblical prophets who at times were hesitant to share the message given to them by God for fear of rejection or retaliation.

Others will refer to prophetic preaching simply as preaching that comes from the prophetic books of the Bible, regardless of the theological application, or the hermeneutic interpretation. If you preach from Isaiah, Daniel, Ezekiel, or the like, regardless of your message, you are being "prophetic." However, as stated prior, I understand prophetic preaching to be proclamation born from the internal reckoning of one's soul and social location in the context of community, resulting in the announcement of God-desired alternatives to systems and ways of being affecting God's creation. This proclamation calls us to commit to such God-desired alternatives with countercultural consciousness, courage, and care.

In *The Politics of Jesus*,[3] Hendricks clearly identifies the function of the prophetic office. Hendricks says,

The primary task of the biblical prophets was not foretelling, but forth-telling in God's name. As forth-tellers, prophets functioned as spokespersons for God who were commissioned to oppose the oppression and collective unrighteousness—that is injustice—of those in positions of power and authority. Foretelling is an integral part of biblical prophecy, but it is the lesser part. It articulates the events, including punishments, that are destined to occur if the truths of forth-telling are ignored and social injustices continue unchecked.[4]

This definition offered by Hendricks helps us to see the foundational concerns of prophetic responsibility. A deeper look will also reveal that prophetic preaching is not just complaining about conditions. While it is important to lift the concerns that deserve complaint, the complaint cannot be the only concern. An alternative reality, born out of an authentic connection to the Creator, and lenses on current conditions, must be spoken by the prophet or prophetic proclaimer in a way that offers hope, and proclaims that what there *is* is not *all* there is. Another way of looking at this is to say that it is frustratingly futile to always be *against* something but never be *for* something. Prophetic preaching does not only speak against the current reality. Prophetic preaching also speaks forth the God-desired alternative reality for God's creation. The prophet is not only clear of the reality he or she is preaching against, but the prophet is also confident in the possibility of the reality for which she or he is advocating. Such clarity and confidence comes forth from the prophet's connection with the Creator who has expanded the vision of the prophet.

Naturally, various practitioners have points of convergence and points of departure when defining prophetic preaching. When describing and defining what prophetic preaching is, Leslie D. Callahan, pastor of the St. Paul Baptist Church of Philadelphia, Pennsylvania, states, "I would define prophetic preaching as preaching that takes into consideration the entirety of human life and thriving and that centers this holistic vision of human living and thriving as integral to the will of God."[5] According to Callahan, prophetic preaching is not just about preaching social ills. In her words, that's sociology. But prophetic preaching must contain a human-to-divine component as well as a human-to-human component. These must be brought into connection and conversation in order to engage in prophetic preaching.

Jeremiah A. Wright, Jr., pastor emeritus of Trinity United Church of Christ in Chicago, considers prophetic preaching to be "preaching that speaks a word of judgment and a word of grace. It has a human and divine component."[6] In particular, preaching prophetically, according to Dr. Wright, requires that one speak the word to people from God's point of view, not human's point of view. Wright and Callahan both intentionally note the human-to-divine component of prophetic preaching.

Frederick Douglass Haynes, III, pastor of the Friendship West Baptist Church in Dallas, Texas, says:

> Prophetic preaching is speaking truth to power while, at the same time, energizing the powerless with alternative possibilities. In unpacking what I have to say, that on one hand, speaking truth to power, it's addressing the issues that structures of power have in place that abort the possibilities of the powerless. It's consciousness-raising. At the

same time, it's empowering the powerless with again a vision of preferred possibilities, alternative possibilities, so that, as Zan Holmes would say, the congregation then becomes the prophetic witness in the community, hearing the message, speaking truth to power, and empowering the powerless.[7]

Father Michael Louis Pfleger, pastor of the St. Sabina Parish in Chicago, considers prophetic preaching to be that which *"proclaims an unsettling, uncomfortable, conscious gospel."*[8]

Again, it is clear that no definition of prophetic preaching has completely been accepted by all. In just the few definitions offered above, there are points of commonality and points of departure. In her book, *Prophetic Preaching*,[9] Leonora Tubbs Tisdale attempted to nail down a definition of prophetic preaching through the perspectives of practitioners and scholars. After considering and conversing with a number of them, instead of nailing down one definition, Tisdale wisely is comfortable maintaining the tension presented in all of the definitions gathered. She therefore presents seven hallmarks of prophetic preaching. Prophetic preaching: (1) is rooted in biblical witness, (2) is countercultural and challenges the status quo, (3) is concerned with evils of present social order and is often more focused on corporate and public issues than on individual and personal concerns, (4) requires the preacher to name what is not of God in the world and what God will bring to pass in a new reality, (5) offers hope of a new day to come and the promise of liberation to God's oppressed people, (6) incites courage in hearers, and (7) requires a heart that breaks with the things that break God's heart.[10]

These seven hallmarks succinctly explain prophetic preaching and its purpose. When looking at the definitions offered by practitioners, and the hallmarks offered by Tisdale, it is evident, but still needs to be said, that prophetic preaching is neither popular nor easily and readily embraced by hearers. Prophetic preaching will not only challenge the agenda of the powers that be, but also the hidden agenda of the people. Put differently, the alternative reality advocated for by prophetic preaching does not only hold powers accountable, but people as well. Prophetic preaching shines a bright light into the dark areas of systems as well as hearts. It can be uncomfortable, but it is vital to lead the people into the *kingdom* of God, one that emulates God's character rather than human desires.

CONCLUSION

Prophetic preaching sounds an alarm to at once warn the masses that something is wrong, while also heralding to the masses a word of hope and help. A preacher's devotional life and connection to the Creator is essential. Therefore, prophetic preaching requires the preacher to remain connected to the central surveillance system of the Creator in order to discern when, where, and how to sound said alarm.

The task of defining prophetic preaching is quite complex. In this chapter alone, we have been exposed to many definitions, with some noted consistencies, and differences. I define prophetic preaching as proclamation born from the internal reckoning of one's soul and social location in the context of community, resulting in the announcement of God-desired alternatives to systems and ways of being affecting God's creation. Prophetic preaching calls us to commit to such God-desired alternatives with countercultural consciousness, courage, and care. I'd encourage you to not only review definitions and hallmarks offered in this chapter, but also construct your own definition of prophetic preaching.

With the outlined hallmarks in this chapter and definitions in mind, we turn our attention to approaches to prophetic preaching. We now look to the precursors of prophetic preaching, beginning with the preacher.

QUESTIONS TO CONSIDER

1. How would you define prophetic preaching?

2. What are the common concepts of prophetic preaching of which you have been made aware?

3. What are the seven hallmarks of prophetic preaching as outlined by Leonora Tubbs Tisdale?

4. What is the definition of prophetic preaching expressed by the author of this book?

NOTES

1. Obery Hendricks, *The Politics of Jesus: Rediscovering the True Revolutionary Nature of the Teachings of Jesus and how They Have Been Corrupted* (New York: Doubleday, 2006).

2. Ibid., 27.

3. Obery Hendricks, *The Politics of Jesus: Rediscovering the True Revolutionary Nature of the Teachings of Jesus and how They Have Been Corrupted* (New York: Doubleday, 2006).

4. Ibid.

5. Callahan, Leslie. Interviewed by Reginald Williams, Jr. Phone Interview for *Moving the Masses: The Role of Prophetic Preaching in the Formation of a Prophetic Congregation*, Virginia Union University, Unpublished Doctoral Project Document for Doctor of Ministry, August 17, 2016.

6. Wright, Jr., Jeremiah A. Interviewed by Reginald W. Williams, Jr. Phone Interview for *Moving the Masses: The Role of Prophetic Preaching in the Formation of*

a Prophetic Congregation, 2017, Virginia Union University, Unpublished Doctoral Project Document for Doctor of Ministry, August 18, 2016.

7. Haynes III., Frederick D. Interviewed by Reginald Williams, Jr. Telephone Interview for *Moving the Masses: The Role of Prophetic Preaching in the Formation of a Prophetic Congregation,* 2017, Virginia Union University, Unpublished Doctoral Project Document for Doctor of Ministry, August 24, 2016.

8. Ibid.

9. Loretta Tubbs Tisdale, *Prophetic Preaching: A Pastoral Approach* (Louisville, KY: Westminster John Knox, 2010), Kindle Edition.

10. Ibid., 9–10.

CHAPTER 2

PRECURSORS TO PROPHETIC PREACHING

Whenever you let someone else tell your story,
they will get it wrong every time.
—REV. DR. JEREMIAH A. WRIGHT, JR.

STORYING

Chancellor Williams, at the beginning of his book *The Destruction of Black Civilization*,[1] tells the Sumerian legend of a traveler who asked an old man as he was traveling, "What became of the Black people of Sumer?"[2] Ancient records show the people were Black and brilliant. The Sumerians invented cuneiform writing systems seventy-five years before hieroglyphics. The Sumerians invented mathematics using the six- and ten-number systems, which enabled them then to invent the clock with its sixty seconds, sixty minutes, twelve hours, and twelve-month calendar. They invented military, legal, and administrative systems. "What happened to these Black and brilliant people?" asked the traveler. "Ah," the old man sighed. "They lost their history, so they died."[3]

Prophetic preaching requires the preacher to remember their personal story and their people's story so that neither they nor the people will die. Remembering is not simply recalling, but re-membering, or putting the memory together again, in a way that gives meaning to moments and movements. Prophetic preaching is literally a matter of life or death for the preacher and the people. In this chapter, I argue that a seminal starting point to prophetic preaching requires one to engage in the process of what I term as storying. Storying is not simply telling a story or illuminating an idea or illustration. While stories and illustrations are important insertions into the sermonic moment that enable people to see themselves in the sermon, that is not the primary concern or purpose of storying in prophetic preaching.

I define *storying* as critical reflection on the meaning of our journey, by excavating and recovering our personal-cultural memory, in order to experience one's existence freely and authentically. My definition of *storying* is heavily influenced by Fernando A. Cascante-Gomez's definition of countercultural autobiography. In the article *Countercultural Autobiography: Stories from The Underside and Education for Justice,*[4] Gomez defines the literary concept as "the interpretive reading of particular moments in the social life of a person who identifies himself or herself with a particular discriminated and/or dominated group in any given society. It is used as a way to voice unjust or oppressive realities suffered within institutional and societal contexts with the ultimate goal of promoting full social inclusion and social justice within and among co-existing diverse human communities."[5] In *Countercultural Autobiography,*[6] Gomez accurately asserts that biography and autobiography are mostly used as teaching tools to help people

23

"acquire educational skills, and to make meaning of our life stories rather than to seek justice."[7]

Storying, then, is not just a biographical retelling of events of a person's life. Storying is a reflection on the meaning of such personal-cultural events, in the context of a socio-cultural framework that gives rise to the events in the life of not only that person but their people as well. The goal is to reflect on the events, which come out of such a socio-cultural framework, in order to challenge and transform that context into one of justice, freedom, and authentic living. Therefore, *storying* is not only the story of a person, but of the people. Storying not only looks at the details of moments and events: storying sets those moments and events into a contextual framework in order to give greater understanding and meaning to those moments and events as part of the journey of person and people.

In this way, it is also helpful to think of storying as engaging in Sankofa. The Akan people of Ghana West Africa have a symbol called the Sankofa bird. The Sankofa symbol is a bird that looks back, grabbing the egg that symbolizes life, while moving forward. It looks back to properly appropriate its past, to move into the future.

The meaning of the symbol is simply that it is impossible to move forward in life unless you know where you've been. In other words, sometimes you've got to look back to move forward. At its essence, this is what storying seeks to accomplish. Storying is an essential component of prophetic preaching for the prophetic preacher. Storying empowers the expression that comes forth to come from a place of authenticity.

The prophetic preacher must be intentional about not only storying their own personal story, but storying the people, and storying the period in which they exist. As I write this book, the movement for Black lives continues to shape the lenses through which many in Black America and the world are looking. Too many humans have been turned into hashtags through state-sponsored violence in the form of modern-day paramilitary forces occupying our communities. From Emmett Till to Breonna Taylor, to George Floyd and Rekia Boyd, to LaQuan McDonald, to Sandra Bland, to Freddie Gray, to Korryn Gaines, to Atatianna Jefferson, the names are all too many, and all too familiar. What is even more common is the fact that these names are also symbolic for names that never make it to the news, never have the benefit of a camera phone to capture their condition but experience the same sadistic treatment at the hands of unethical law enforcement. In 2020, Jacob Blake, who was shot seven times in the back by officers in Kenosha, Wisconsin, was informed that none of those officers would face prosecution. While Derrick Chauvin was found guilty for the murder of George Floyd by means of a knee to the neck, the names of women and men far too many to count are subjected to subhuman treatment, which also sucks the life from them. During the writing of this book, the pandemics of COVID 1619[8] and COVID-19 are ravishing communities throughout this country and world. Black and brown bodies and communities in America and the world over continue to be under-resourced, and over-policed. During the writing of this book, the world has witnessed an attempted coup, instigated by a sitting president in his last days of office, based on notions of privilege, entitlement, and faulty claims of voter fraud. As I write this book, racism, sexism, homophobia, ageism, ableism, and other "isms," and "phobias," plague the planet supported by individuals and institutions who benefit from the continued maintenance of said "isms" and "phobias."

The preacher / prophet must remain connected to the central surveillance system in order to interpret and story the times by giving meaning to the milieu in which we find ourselves. This storying must thread its way from the preacher to the people. Dr. Itihare Toure[9] reminds us that making time to recall our stories is an essential component of dealing with trauma. Storying reminds us that we have what we need to survive. Storying also will assist those coming after us to use our storying as a survival guide when future issues arise.

In *Joy Unspeakable*, Barbara Holmes makes an important connection between contemplation (of which I argue storying is an expression), activism, and practice. She speaks from her own story by stating, "We are a family of storytellers. We always knew who we were because elders shared their 'recollections' at the kitchen table. Stories include harrowing escapes, mysterious instances of divine intervention, and a matter-of-fact inclusion of personal achievements interlaced with visitations from the spirit realm."[10]

Further, Holmes explores African-centered midrash through griosh.[11] "In the motherland, griots retained the memories through the public recitation of stories. Without these gatherings, the tradition began to wither. When the community could not gather, and the griots could not keep the memories, they ensconced their own stories in the biblical narratives. Because slavery severed extended family ties, each communal group had to have their own methods of maintaining the corporate memory."[12]

The storytelling expressed by Holmes is at its foundation what I have termed storying. Storying empowers one to speak from an authentic center of power that cannot be found in comparisons and imitations.

Storying is a primary precursor to prophetic preaching. In addition, it is important to be aware of the lenses through which one looks as they engage in this task of prophetic preaching. Now we move from storying as an approach, to the lenses through which we look as prophetic preachers.

SEEING

At times, upon completion of sermons preached in class, Dr. Jones would utter the words, "You have helped us." Students of Dr. Jones reading this may possibly have a post-traumatic reaction to just reading those words and hearing his bold baritone voice through the intercom of eternity, as those words are read. This is because what remained to be seen, upon his utterance, was whether Dr. Jones deemed that the sermon helps us to see what to do or what not to do. There were also times when he would ask, "What did you see?" This question would compel the students to share what they discerned as they constructed the sermon presented in class. Prior to us delving into the method that connects the authenticity of the person with the proclamation, I offer three lenses through which the prophetic preacher must peer in order to answer Dr. Jones' question, What did you see? These lenses give a frame to what the prophetic preacher sees, and subsequently says on behalf of God to the people of God.

SELF

"Social justice starts in the bedroom." This assertion of the dearly departed, wise, wonderful, womanist ethicist theologian preacher and professor Dr. Katie Geneva

Canon reminds us that what we do in terms of justice begins in the most intimate places of our being. Such is the case also with the preacher. Preaching, and especially prophetic preaching, requires that one take internal inventory as one brings the whole of who they are to the preaching moment. In other words, it is vitally important for one to know their own story to help illumine the lessons of the story they see in the scripture. However, it will not begin if one does not engage in intentional internal investigation.

The lens of self is the first lens. When we are not living through our own lenses, we cannot really ascertain what's authentic. As previously stated, Howard Thurman's "Sound of the Genuine" address really expresses the importance of the lens of self. Later on in the same address, Thurman says:

> There is in you something that waits and listens for the sound of the genuine in yourself and sometimes, there is so much traffic going on in your minds, so many different kinds of signals, so many vast impulses floating through your organism that go back thousands of generations, long before you were even a thought in the mind of creation, and you are buffeted by these and, in the midst of all of this, you have got to find out what your name is. Who are you? How does the sound of the genuine come through to you? . . . The sound of the genuine is flowing through you.[13]

We must be intentional about discovering the sound of the genuine in ourselves in our efforts to engage in prophetic preaching. Otherwise, one may be found guilty of prophetic fraud. Discovering the sound of the genuine in ourselves requires a deep dive of self-discovery, with the Sankofa sensibilities found in storying. I argue this voyage of discovery will move us to look in at least two areas, your people and your person.

PEOPLE

The story of the slave ship *La Amistad* is a true story that every person should know. It is the story of African people living under the sadistic, satanic, devastating, and demonic condition of chattel slavery. This story is the story of those who had been captured and chained and were being transported as property to lands unknown. On the way, these Africans, who had been "seasoned" and sold, decided that they were not going to take the inhumane, abusive treatment anymore. And so they rose up, and took over the ship, and took over the enslavers who were intending to sell them for service. In the movie *Amistad*, which recounts the events surrounding *La Amistad*, there is a pivotal scene that illustrates the importance of the prophetic preacher seeing self through the lens of your people and their history. The scene is a conversation between the attorney, played by Matthew McConaughey, and the African named Cinque, played by Djimon Hounsou. The attorney, who is assigned by and aligned with the abolitionists, poses one question that forces Cinque into deep thought and reflection. The attorney asks Cinque: "How did you get here?"

How did you get here? For many Africans in the Americas and the diaspora, that is a daunting and haunting question that perplexes us because of the sick, sad, and sordid history of chattel slavery. Chattel slavery tore families apart, sold loved ones away into a brutal system, and many were never seen again; chattel slavery separated tribesmen and women from those in their villages. However, as a general measure, we have found there to be cultural unity in some African ethnicities. This is critical to understand because it reminds all who care to listen that even the most heinous of efforts to divide and destroy an entire people's culture through evil acts, was rendered insufficient, both then and now. Much more information can be found on this very important subject by reading such books as *The Cultural Unity of Black Africa*[14] by Cheikh Diop, *Africanisms in American Culture*[15] by Joseph Holloway, and *Christian Theology and AfroCultures: Toward an Afrikan Centered Hermeneutic* by Mark Lomax.[16] As such, throughout the Diaspora, there have been Africanisms that survived and religious syncretism grounded in African-derived religions. I offer this as part of a general lens of seeing the self as well as one's cultural origin and influence on religion, particularly for Africans in America and throughout the Diaspora.

The late Asa Hilliard, the brilliant African-centered educational psychologist, says that too often we get caught up in seeing the history of our people as an episode. An episode is just one piece of an entire puzzle, and just one part of a whole. And too often we look at our history through episodic eyes, lifting up certain predicaments or people in our history. For instance, especially around Black History Month, we tend to focus historical lenses on the episode of chattel slavery, as if we began in slavery. The truth of the matter is that slavery was just an episode, not the entire epic of our people. African people were beautiful and brilliant before, during, and after the sick system of slavery. African people created civilizations, built pyramids, discovered forms of farming and animal husbandry, and created academic institutions and libraries from which the world came to learn. To focus on one episode, without acknowledging the epic of African people, is disingenuous, and does not speak to the full epic of a people.

We will look through the same episodic eyes when it comes to certain people. We will name a Martin Luther King, Jr., and a Sojourner Truth. We'll name a Marcus Garvey and a Harriet Tubman as exemplars of our experience. However, to look through the lens of a people encourages us not to get stuck in the episodes of our people but to look at the epic of our people. The episode, or calling one person's name, is just part of the whole. The epic is the whole story. When we just concentrate solely on the episodes of our people, then we fall into the game of singling out certain people and singling out predicaments. When we single out certain people and certain predicaments, then adversaries attempt to choose "approved" heroes in an attempt to dictate what is acceptable to the dominant culture's pallet.

Further, when this is internalized, there is the tendency to encourage children and others to be the next this, and the next that, instead of inviting and encouraging them to be the best of who they are, because they are the links in a long-running chain of fruitful and prolific people. When we buy into the episodic separation and lifting up of only a few people, that invites definition, division, and denigration of a people. This is exactly what white supremacy does. It seeks to separate and then validate based on white supremacist conceptions of what should be and what shouldn't be. Looking through the authentic eye of your people is not just about a few people whose names can be called during Black History Month. Looking through the authentic eyes of a people is about the epic of a people who have done the most with the least on this planet. When given blues, African people made music. When given hopelessness, African people made hip-hop. When given pain, African people turned it into poetry. When given sorrow, African people sang the spirituals. History is not just about the episodes of a people, but the epic of a whole people.

In addition to the epic of a people, there are those who may dig deeper into the history of their own families to mark meaning and movements that matter to the importance of their people. Some may interview elders in the family or community to get information as to how they got where they are.

For instance, for many who live "Up South" (a term referring to those who migrated north, or up, from the South), it would be interesting to discover how and why their people left the South to come to the north. This type of exploration may help a family better understand their unique story individually and collectively. Isabel Wilkerson beautifully captures this leaderless movement called the Great Migration, in her book *The Warmth of Other Suns*.[17]

Discovery of your people in general and your family in particular can help give a lens into why you are who you are, as you are, regardless of who you are. This is an important part of seeing. Many in recent years have taken to instruments like ancestry.com and other means that attempt to trace a person's origins based on DNA taken from a swab. While I think it's a good tool to use, I would invite you to also read the fine print to ascertain ownership or other issues that may arise as a result of your use of this service.

Here are a few questions that can begin the practice of self-reflection.

- Where are you from?
- Who are your people?
- What is the story of those from whom you come?
- What is the history of your people?
- What are the tragedies and triumphs of your people (family of origin or community) that you can pass on?
- What are the significant connections of your story to your people that make you who you are?
- What are the personal and people pains that are intricately interwoven into your story?

PERSON

As we look through the lenses of the self, the epic of your people is an important informational component. Equally important is the information gained by looking at the person. I'm advocating for those who would engage in prophetic preaching to explore the lens of self not only through your people but also your person.

If you're reading this, it is quite likely that you own and operate a smartphone. Due to technological advances, many smartphones include a feature called a GPS, which stands for Global Positioning System. The Global Positioning System keeps the holder of the smartphone aware of where they are located anywhere in the world. The system is facilitated by a satellite, which is not apparent to our eyes, that is connected to a chip inside of the phone. In essence that satellite that we cannot see can see us. Not only does it see us, but it helps us to see ourselves. And not only does it see us and help us see ourselves, the GPS helps us to get a glimpse of the destination that has been programmed. And, notably, the system helps us to course correct when we have veered away from our peculiar and particular path. Have you heard it scream out, "Recalculating"? When you make a wrong turn or you don't follow the course, the GPS automatically reconfigures a route to still get you to the intended destination. In essence, the GPS is an instrument that enhances our awareness as to our current location on the way to our destination.

The Enneagram of Personality is a comprehensive psycho-spiritual GPS, grafted from the wisdom of ancient Egyptian desert clerics, which helps people to locate themselves. The enneagram is more in-depth and layered than a Myers-Briggs personality type assessment, or other personality indices. The enneagram, when experienced in-depth, helps people understand how they see the world and manage emotions. The enneagram is not an instrument to put you in a box, but to help you understand the box you are in already. In addition to accessing a therapist, people serious about deeply diving into who they are would do well to engage the enneagram as a tool. Again, the enneagram is a map of human nature, which helps us to see who we are already. The Enneagram Institute[18] is a great site to begin the journey of exploring the enneagram. The image[19] below indicates the nine types of personality mapping, offered by this ancient wisdom instrument. These one-word descriptors can be expanded

into four-word sets of traits. Keep in mind that these are merely highlights and do not represent the full spectrum of each type.

To begin exploring this instrument, go to a number of websites that offer free or low-cost enneagram assessments. While the free assessments are good, of course the low-cost assessments are much more in-depth. Just enter "enneagram" in the search engine on your browser, and you will find a selection of sites from which to choose. After completing the enneagram, the site should inform you of your dominant type. From there, the journey into self-exploration can begin.

The enneagram differs from other assessments in that the enneagram delves beneath the personality to get to the source and soul of the real person. The enneagram empowers us to explore the episodes of our lives that have experienced both wounding and wonder. It further empowers us to acknowledge old and false narratives, while offering the opportunity through awareness to create new narratives in which to walk. The enneagram gets at the true self that lies beneath personality. The true self is the soul of the person beneath all of the masks and makeup. This search into the true self reveals not only the highs, but also the challenges. Herein is the power of the enneagram as opposed to other personality-driven instruments. By raising awareness as to our own challenges, the enneagram can help us grow to not allowing unconscious activities or expressions to control our actions. The enneagram empowers us to engage, embrace, and accept the whole of our true selves created by God. Some have even noted the enneagram's nine types as the nine faces of the soul.[21] Moreover, the enneagram empowers one who utilizes it to accept themselves and accept others for who they are, and where they are on life's journey. Juanita Rasmus says it best when she states that, "The Enneagram shows us how each of us reflect an aspect of God's character. Our challenge is to show the image of God without our ego taking over."[22] All of these examples go into understanding yourself as the person as you explore your epic and story. All of this shapes the lenses through which we look at ourselves. The awareness this brings is immeasurable and a great start to empowering others.

With vulnerability and transparency, I will share that I am a Type 2 on the enneagram spectrum. In storying myself, I came to understand that as a 2, I learned to help and please others, even if it was to my own detriment, because attending to my personal needs made me feel as if I was being selfish. Type 2s like me will attest that this stems from childhood frames of feeling loved only when they were pleasing or helping others. Love became defined as helping others, even if that same help was not reciprocated, causing this 2 to feel unloved. Therefore, I felt like I had to give endlessly in order to be embraced, which frequently left me feeling empty and unloved. The other side to this continuous giving is that there is an unconscious expectation attached. This is because the 2 feels a sense of pride when others are dependent on them to give. It follows then that the 2 subconsciously expects that those she or he helps will give back freely to him in the same or a similar way. When this doesn't occur, 2s can be silently resentful, because they have not expressed their needs and have not had them met. Under stress, Type 2s can then move to some of the characteristics of an unhealthy 8, which includes being angry, manipulative, and believing others owe them while somatizing their pain. Such operation in stressful situations speaks to the false narrative that does not have to encompass a Type 2.

On my healing journey, I have learned that as a Type 2, I don't have to give to be loved; I am worthy of love simply because of who I am. Love is not transactional, but unconditional. In this way, my journey has given me awareness and approval to love myself, all sides of myself. This awareness also empowers me to keep those shadow sides in check and recognize when they rear their heads. This awareness also empowers me to live a more authentic existence, a very important step in proclaiming prophetic messages. Living in this level of awareness and authenticity empowers the preacher to unapologetically bring all of who they are to the preaching moment, and the practices included in the preparation for the same. We begin with this self-lens in order to embrace our own sacred text, even as we prepare to interpret and proclaim from a sacred text.

As an example, understanding my place on the enneagram spectrum has empowered me to understand and embrace why the matters of identity and justice are so important to me and show up in my preaching. Healthy Type 2s have empathy and care for others. This is why it pains them to see injustices, be they systemic, institutional, or levied on individuals. However, as a Type 2, my healing journey has also shown that my identity is not up for debate, because I am worthy of care, concern, compassion, and dignity just as I am. As I have surveyed much of my preaching, the themes of identity and justice come to the fore. I used to be concerned about it, as I didn't want to be typecast or pigeonholed. However, understanding that this is who I am, and the lenses through which I look, has emboldened me to be unapologetic about who I am and why.

Whatever theme, or topic, I preach will in some way, directly or indirectly, address matters of authenticity and identity as they relate to God's purpose and plan for God's creation. This awareness has emanated from intentional work with my therapist, use and study of the enneagram, and the awareness that comes from storying. Such awareness gives a great framework to my unique and authentic focus, unapologetically. The enneagram is a powerful tool that can empower the preacher to uncover all of who the preacher is, in an effort to live more authentically.

So how does this lens empower the prophetic preacher? The power of the enneagram is in the awareness that it provides as a lens into self. It helps us see much better. Employing and embracing the enneagram can give people awareness into their human nature and the factors that empower them to operate at their best or worst selves and why. This is why it is a psycho-social spiritual wisdom instrument. It empowers us through awareness, to live into the best versions of ourselves as God created us to be, while remaining aware of factors that compromise the same. This does not mean that the preacher has to relay all of the details about themselves and their experiences. The preaching moment is not to be used to bleed on people or to share in the preaching moment what should be shared in the office of a therapist. However, understanding the "why" of ourselves will not only empower us to story ourselves, but to also strengthen ourselves. Moreover, if one can be clear and honest about the complexities and contradictions of themselves, they are much more empowered to do the same as it relates to scripture and society. This honest approach empowers the prophetic preacher with a power of authenticity that may have the result of moving masses.

For the purpose of engaging and excavating one's own personal part of looking through the self-lens, I highly encourage walking through the enneagram. For those who engage in such, there is a plethora of resources to help you on the journey to yourself. Foundational texts for those interested in getting a general introduction include *The Enneagram Made Easy* and *The Enneagram: A Christian Perspective*. You can also go to https://www.enneagraminstitute.com to learn more about the enneagram.

SCRIPTURE

The next lens to look through in the journey toward seeing as a means to authentically utilize storying in prophetic preaching is the lens of scripture.

In the critically acclaimed movie *Birth of a Nation*, the story of Nat Turner is told. The film shows Nat's master at the behest of a local clergyman, manipulating Nat's gifts as a preacher to preach a slave theology to other enslaved Africans. For this deed, Nat's master would get a pretty penny. However, as time went on, Nat would appropriate other scriptures—those outside of the prescribed scriptures that would further the status quo. In fact, one of the most compelling scenes revealed that Nat knew scripture just as well as the conniving clergyman and was able to go head-to-head with the clergyman until Nat was knocked out by his master and whipped. The scripture quoted by the conniving Christian colonizer was used in a way to justify Nat and his people's continued confinement and dehumanization. However, from the same Bible, Nat quoted scriptures that justified and affirmed the humanity and authenticity of Nat and his people. From the same Bible emerged two different interpretations that underscored the fact that there are some who depend on the Bible as god and others who are connected to the God of the Bible. Many have and continue to use the Bible to push an agenda of domination, not liberation. Such an approach reveals that you can make the Bible say what you want the Bible to say for your own purposes. Put differently, there are some who will use the Bible as a weapon of mass deception, destruction, and dehumanization as long as it preserves their privilege and supports a god made in their image.

Such a lens will embolden deacons in a church to sing hymns in the morning, then leave church and lynch Black people on the same afternoon. This is also what we see in our modern-day context when some white western evangelicals will use scripture to justify their own bigoted beliefs, supporting racist presidents and politicians, while demonizing a movement for all Black lives. However, there are others who will look to the God of the Bible for courage, strength, and hope in the midst of a world gone mad to bring about an alternative reality. Some will see the liberating lyrics of scripture and employ those lyrics as lessons for liberation. These are just two interpretations emerging from the same Bible.

The scene in *Birth of a Nation*, and the scenes we see playing over our screens on a daily basis, reveal that a proper view of scripture is necessary to faithfully and prophetically proclaim the gospel.

It has been posited that in reading the sacred text, one brings their sacred text to the sacred text. In other words, your lived experiences are sacred and these experiences make up the story that authenticates your existence. You came from a context with content shaped by that context; your environment and settings shaped how you viewed certain realities. As such, your sacred text garnered from that context will color how you experience and/or exegete the sacred text from which we preach. The same is the case with this sacred text and scripture we call the Bible.

However, the sacred text called the Bible must be studied and explored to understand its context, and thereby to understand its content. The book *Misreading Scripture with Western Eyes*[23] is an excellent text to help us understand how we can put our cultural blinders on the interpretation of scripture and make it say things it never was meant to say. Any faithful preacher, when exegeting and excavating the meaning of the messages written thousands of years ago, must take seriously the context out of which the content comes forth.

The contextual framework in which scripture was written is an essential element to understanding how to properly proclaim a prophetic message. Jerome Ross, Hebrew Bible professor at the Samuel DeWitt Proctor School of Theology, helps us with his essay in *Born to Preach*.[24] According to Ross in the essay titled "The Cultural Affinity Between the Ancient Yahwist and African Americans: A Hermeneutic for Homiletics," the Yahwists were dominated by the superpower nations during the biblical period, with the exception of the reign of David Solomon. In fact, they existed under six types of oppression at different points: Egyptian, Assyrian, Babylonian, Persian, Greek, and Roman oppression. To live under one of those six different types of oppression meant at least four things. Living under oppression meant that a people were exposed to the imposed requirements of the suzerain of the vassal state: (1) forced acceptance of their administrative arrangements, (2) payment of tribute, (3) forced acceptance of their religions, and (4) unconditional loyalty, that is, no foreign alliances.[25]

Looking at scripture through lenses that acknowledges and affirms these realities under which the people of that time lived is essential to preparing and preaching any sermon of any kind utilizing that very text.

SOCIETY

In addition to seeing self and scripture authentically, finally, the prophetic preacher must also know how to look through the lens of society. I never met my great-grandfather Rev. George Hambrick. I am told he was an associate pastor at the First Church of Deliverance under the leadership of Rev. Clarence Cobb on the South Side of Chicago. I am also told that in the morning when he came downstairs to begin his day, he would carry three things with him: his Bible, his newspaper, and his gun.

While this combination he carried may appear comical at first glance, I'd like to think that my great-grandfather's "carrying case" was instructive and demonstrated his awareness of his context. He knew the importance of looking at society with the benefit of scripture as well as living in society with the benefit of at least attempting to live in a space of security. Put differently, it appears that he knew the importance of using his self and scriptural lenses as two of many interpretive tools for analyzing society.

The prophetic preacher must be aware of what is going on in society. In other words, the prophetic preacher must be able to ascertain the stories of the people to whom they are preaching, and how those stories lean against, are limited by, or are lacerated by, the structures of society. This requires listening to the lives of those to whom we preach.

But in a deeper sense, it requires listening to life. This includes but is not limited to issues that arise in the public square. Preachers must be readers, and lifelong learners, so as to be able to serve this present age. In the listening and learning, the prophetic preacher must be able to give deep analysis of the times in which the people live in order to accurately and adequately interpret the times for the people who are living through these times.

That is, what are the structures, institutions, policies, practices, and people, that are affecting the people's stories who will be listening to your sermon? How are you helping the people interpret this moment and move to a future intended by God? What mental models, systemic analyses, and priestly presence are you offering to help your people read the times? This is where the prophet must have keen social analysis to ascertain where the injustices on a systemic level are attacking the stories of the people to whom we are preaching. The prophet must study society and have mental models and investigative tools and resources that give the prophet the perspective that will help the prophet to see and say that which says the Lord because of what is seen in society. This will require the prophet to do more than just study the Bible. Attention must be given to an interdisciplinary study of politics, economics, sociology, anthropology, and other disciplines that give the prophet the tools and eyes to interpret meaning and movement *with* the people, and not just *for* the people. Prophets must be readers, and prophets must read other prophets, of the pulpit, pavement, and everything in between. Placing prophets of various disciplines in conversation through intellectual curiosity, and intentional imagination can be enlightening to the one wanting to practice prophetic preaching. Particularly in times of social unrest, it would behoove the prophetic preacher to pay attention to the artist in the community, as many times artists have an ability to authentically and artistically articulate the pathos of the people, the longing of the people, and the desired progress of the people. In times of social unrest, and in times of social upheaval, it is the artists and creatives of our culture that also offer prophetic utterances.

Poets like Claude McKay will release poetry out of pain that says, "If we must die, let it not be like hogs hunted and penned in an inglorious spot."[26] Maya Angelou will tell you why the caged bird sings.[27] Writers like Toni Morrison will offer characters like Baby Suggs in her novel *Beloved* who encourages enslaved to love their flesh because others don't love their flesh. Or James Baldwin's *The Fire Next Time* and *Nobody Knows My Name* can inform the preacher of people's need for liberation. August Wilson wrote ten plays on each decade of Black life in the twentieth century—within his words are the heartbeat of a people crying out. The prophetic preacher would do well to be informed by those cries. Creatives in visual arts like Basquiat, Kehinde Wiley, Kara Walker, and Kerry James Marshall have also fueled revolution based on their usage of the lens to capture society on canvas.

Musical artists have also helped fuel the revolution. African ancestors on plantations were creatives in cotton fields, crooning songs that sounded good to Massa, but were code language that told slaves when the Underground Railroad was leaving. That's what the lyrics "Swing low, sweet chariot, coming for to carry me home" were about. They had songs that gave meaning to messages. So when they would sing *Couldn't Hear Nobody*

Pray, that is believed to have meant that the previous night the people in the house couldn't hear them having worship in the brush arbors and hush arbors.

Much of the movement of the 1960s and 1970s to propel Black people from self-hatred to loving the skin they were in and fighting against anything that deterred that effort was fueled by musical artists such as Curtis Mayfield, Gladys Knight & The Pips, The Chi-Lites, the Staples Singers, and Stevie Wonder. They provided fuel for the fighting. As Black music evolved, it continued to focus on consciousness-raising. I am personally a child of the hip-hop generation, having been raised in the golden era of hip-hop. Artists like Grandmaster Flash & Melle Mel, Run DMC, Queen Latifah, MC Lyte, Public Enemy, and others are just a few of the artists who helped to put in lyrics that expressed the longing of the people. Kendrick Lamar has penned lyrics that have become part of the current soundtrack of the movement for Black lives with his classic *Alright*. During times of social upheaval, artists like Common, Black Thought, Rakim, and others demanded to be heard. Listening to these prophets of the pavement would benefit the prophetic preacher in getting a framework for the longings and the hopes of the people.

The aforementioned are just examples of prophets in the arts. However, placing prophets and scholars in the fields of medicine, education, the arts, theology, sociology, psychology, anthropology, sports, science, agriculture, and other disciplines in conversation with one another will yield insight for the prophetic preacher seeking to proclaim an alternative reality approved by God as opposed to the current reality under which people live.

As we consider this lens of society, placing these prophets, scholars, artists, and others in conversation not only empowers the prophetic preacher to be aware, but also engage in analysis, so that the people can act in a way that seeks to bring about an alternative reality.

Considering the lenses through which to look regarding society, some of the following questions may help.

- What is the sacred text of the stories of the people to whom you are preaching? That is, what are the socioeconomic conditions affecting those to whom you are preaching?
- What is the text of the story of our society? What are the issues and institutions affecting the people the most?
- What are the practices and policies affecting the people the most? How are those effects playing out in the lives of the people to whom you are preaching?
- What is the link in your story, the story of the scripture, and the story of the people to whom you are preaching?
- Preaching and teaching prophetically is incomplete without the ability of the preacher to name and give analysis to the times in which we live, and offer an alternative way of being, living, and the reality that is to come.
- What are the matters of charity, and the matters of justice to which we are to attend?

In tending to matters of society, the preacher cannot afford to fall asleep. It is the preacher who must articulate and give analysis to the times in which we live.

This requires prayer and participation in the political process.

CONCLUSION

In this chapter, we have explored some precursors to prophetic preaching. Storying is a precursor that calls on the preacher to reflect on the meaning of our journey, by excavating our personal-cultural memory, because such exploration is essential for authentic existence. Storying can be thought of as a Sankofa moment, and I argue is a spiritual practice. In addition to storying is the precursory practice of seeing. Seeing requires that we look through the lenses of self, scripture, and society to approach the moment of proclamation with ingenuity and integrity.

QUESTIONS TO CONSIDER

1. What are the precursors to prophetic preaching?
2. What is storying?
3. Name and describe the three lenses through which to look while engaging in prophetic preaching.

NOTES

1. Chancellor Williams, *Destruction of Black Civilization* (Chicago: Third World Press, 1987).

2. Ibid., 15.

3. Ibid., 15.

4. Fernando A. Cascante-Gómez, "Countercultural Autobiography: Stories From The Underside and Education For Justice," *Religious Education* volume #102, no. 3 (Summer 2007): 279–286.

5. Ibid., 286.

6. Ibid., 279.

7. Ibid.

8. 1619 refers to the year it was said Africans were first brought to these shores as enslaved however, other research shows that African people were present on these shores prior to 1619.

9. Itihare Toure is Director of Institutional Research, Planning and Effectiveness at the Interdenominational Theological Center in Atlanta, Georgia.

10. Barbara Holmes, *Joy Unspeakable: Contemplative Practices of The Black Church* (Minneapolis: Fortress Press), Kindle edition location 193 of 2451.

11. Ibid, location 1408 of 2451. *Griosh* is derived from the word griot, referring to African storytellers who were also historians and keepers of cultural memory.

12. Ibid, location 1408 of 2451.

13. Howard Thurman, "The Sound of the Genuine," Spelman Baccalaureate Address 1980. Published by Indianapolis University Crossings Project, https://www.uindy.edu/eip/files/reflection4.pdf, accessed April 27, 2021.

14. Cheikh A. Diop, *The Cultural Unity of Black Africa: The Domains of Patriarchy and of Matriarchy in Classical Antiquity* (London: Karnak House, 1989).

15. Joseph E. Holloway, *Africanisms in American Culture* (Bloomington: Indiana University Press), 1990.

16. Mark Ogunwale Lomax, *Christian Theology and Africultures: Toward an Afrikan Centered Hermenuetic.* https://btpbase.org/christian-theology-and-afrocultures-toward-an-afrikan-centered-hermeneutic/, accessed January 18, 2021.

17. Isabel Wilkerson, *The Warmth of Other Suns* (New York: Vintage Books, 2014).

18. See https://www.enneagraminstitute.com.

19. "The Enneagram can be seen as a set of nine distinct personality types, with each number on the Enneagram denoting one type. It is common to find a little of yourself in all nine of the types, although one of them should stand out as being closest to yourself. This is your basic personality type. Everyone emerges from childhood with one of the nine types dominating their personality, with inborn temperament and other pre-natal factors being the main determinants of our type. This is one area where most all of the major Enneagram authors agree—we are born with a dominant type. Subsequently, this inborn orientation largely determines the ways in which we learn to adapt to our early childhood environment," https://www.enneagraminstitute.com.

20. See https://www.enneagraminstitute.com.

21. Sandra Maitri, *The Spiritual Dimension of the Enneagram: Nine Faces of the Soul* (New York: Jeremy P. Tarcher / Putnam, 2000).

22. Juanita Rasmus, *Learning to Be: Finding Your Center After the Bottom Falls Out* (Downers Grove, IL: Inter-Varsity Press, 2020).

23. Richards, Professor E. Randolph, and Brandon J. O'Brien, *Misreading Scripture with Western Eyes* (Downers Grove, IL: Inter-Varsity Press, 2012).

24. Ross, Jerome, "The Cultural Affinity Between the Ancient Yahwists and the African Americans: A Hermeneutic for Homiletic" in *Born To Preach: Essays in Honor of The Ministry of Henry & Ella Mitchell*, edited by Samuel K. Roberts, (Valley Forge, PA: Judson Press, 2000).

25. Ibid.

26. Claude McKay, *If We Must Die*, 1919.

27. Maya Angelou, *I Know Why the Caged Bird Sings* (New York: Ballantine Books, 2009).

CHAPTER 3

SERMON DEFINITION & DEFINITIVE CONTENT OF A SERMON

*"Jesus is an interpretive reality,
in need of interpretation."*
—MILES JEROME JONES

DEFINITION OF A SERMON

On Tuesday, September 14, 1999, Miles Jones distributed the course syllabus to anxious and aspiring preachers of the Gospel. On the back of the first page of the syllabus was an article written by James Wall, titled "The Sermon: A Work Of Art." In the opening sentence of the seventh paragraph of that article, these words are recorded: "A sermon, then, must be a statement of faith, drawn from the context of the biblical tradition, and projecting the authentic being of the preacher."

An explanation of this definition, as taught by Dr. Jones, is essential before progressing in our exploration of prophetic preaching and will therefore be the next part of our process in this book.

STATEMENT OF FAITH

As stated in part one of *Moving the Masses*, the sermon's substance does not begin with the scripture, but with the preacher. According to Dr. Jones, "True biblical preaching is primarily declaring a gospel that is experienced, and then using a Bible that is known."[1] Therefore, the sermon as a statement of faith comes from the belief system of the preacher. It is an outgrowth of what the preacher believes to be true. This statement of faith exhibits and indicates the preacher's relationship to and experience with God. It is upon this statement that the preacher unashamedly and unapologetically stands.

DRAWN FROM THE CONTEXT OF THE BIBLICAL TRADITION

DRAWN

The word drawn implies that we are pulling something from something else. Just as water is drawn from the depths of a well, the statement of faith is drawn from the depths of the preacher's soul, relationship with God, and Scripture. Drawing requires work to uncover what is covered in the text. To draw something out of something else implies that we must labor and wrestle with the self and scripture, in order to uncover that which is covered. It is the work of exposing what has been enclosed.

CONTEXT OF

The context of the biblical tradition implies that the text has a context from which the text emanates. Drawing from the context of the biblical tradition requires an understanding of the context in order to really understand the meaning of the text. The text is the meat, while the context is the gravy and onions surrounding the meat to accentuate the meat itself. The origin and meaning are not just glossed off the top of the scripture. Rather the key is getting to the depths of the origin, which then gives the text and context substance that is deeper than the surface.

It is important to faithfully explore the context of the text to not engage in identity theft. In other words, consideration of the context will push the preacher to proclaim what the text says, not what the preacher wants the text to say.

BIBLICAL TRADITION

The tradition becomes the housing for the context but is not a prison from which the tradition cannot escape or be extricated. The tradition is drawn from the context of the time but is not limited to such. It's important to understand the author and the author's original audience to understand the meaning of the text. However, to stay in that tradition renders the word obsolete and irrelevant for today's people. Understanding and drawing from the context of the biblical tradition invites us to draw parallels, extract principles, and discern connections without holding us hostage to that time and place. Herein lies the difference between drawing on tradition and engaging in traditionalism.

In a 2002 interview with *Religion and Ethics Newsweekly*, Robert Michael Franklin quotes Yale historian Jaroslav Pelikan when he says that tradition is the living faith of the dead, but traditionalism is the dead faith of the living.[2] We want to draw from the tradition in order to preach a living word, not a locked-up word.

This is also part of the work of drawing and working to ascertain what is meant by what is said in the scripture.

PROJECTING THE AUTHENTIC BEING OF
THE PREACHER

The statement of faith drawn from the context of the biblical tradition should not be someone else's statement. It should come from the authentic being of the preacher. Projecting the authentic being of the preacher connects us back to the definition of prophetic preaching outlined in chapter 1. As a reminder, prophetic preaching emanates from an internal reckoning of one's soul and social location in the context of community. Out of this reckoning, the authentic being is projected. Only the preacher and God can answer the question of whether the preacher is being authentic or seeking to be acceptable. Authenticity is derived from the root word for authority (*auctorias*), which means to enlarge or amplify. This signifies that there is a strength and power in being yourself that does not come from one being anything other than yourself. In the words of Dr. Jones, again, "God knows who God called." As such, because you have been authorized by God, you are enough! God has authorized you as enough before the foundations of the world. Standing in this authority empowers and emboldens the preacher to be fully who you are in the preaching moment. There is no need to ape or copy anyone else because God has authorized you as being enough. Project your authentic being!

Projecting the authentic being of the preacher means that the sermon ought to be a result of the experience of the preacher with the passage, before the expression through proclamation. This statement of faith should project and portray the authenticity of the preacher. This means that another may influence one, but the preacher cannot copy another or imitate anyone else—otherwise the preaching is inauthentic. It is inevitable that a young preacher who has learned from and listened to his or her pastor or mentor for years may express some of the tendencies heard from said pastor or mentor. This may become a part of them. However, this does not mean that the student copies the teacher, but the teacher has become a part of the student. The work of the student is to take all of whom that student is and lean into the process of sounding like oneself, which is based on the relationship the preacher has with God and the experiences the individual has encountered and observed.

It is this portion of the definition of a sermon that is so essential to the basis of prophetic preaching, as expressed in Chapter 2. In Part 2, we will deal with methodology. That is, we are exploring the intricacies of putting a sermon together. However, methodology is different from authenticity. While the methodology projects how the sermon is put together, authenticity projects how you are put together. At its base, a sermon ought to project how you are put together. This means that the projection of your authenticity should reveal but not be limited to the anatomy of how you think into a sermon, the style that comes from your own substance, the way your words are put together, the way your cadences come forth, and the substance of your own story.

All of this will be influenced by the unique lenses of the preacher and his or her interpretation or lived experience. This is authentic to you, and this is what God wants to express to others through your lenses, to project your authentic being through this sermon. Don't short-change your authenticity. It's an affront to God and it short-changes the people. Again, this is why it is so important to do the internal work of locating yourself—as outlined in Chapter 2.

As one is crafting and constructing a sermon, one must ask: Am I being authentic or trying to be acceptable? Never take for granted the strength and sacred sound of your own authenticity!

DEFINITIVE CONTENT OF A SERMON

Since we have the definition of a sermon, we now turn to the definitive content of a sermon. According to Dr. Jones, the definitive content of a Christian sermon is kerygma. Kerygma is the expression and interpretation of the meaning of the life, death, and resurrection of Jesus Christ. Christian preaching is above all concerned with the imperative of changing lives through the revelation of the power of the gospel, seen in the liberating life of Jesus Christ. Christian preaching cannot just be information or inspiration, but it must also be geared toward transformation rooted in the understanding of Christ. Many times, if the kerygmatic content is the determining factor of the entire sermon, it is saved until the end. However, kerygmatic content can be anywhere in the sermon. With kerygma, the unique experience of the Christ event opens the door to preaching and Christian proclamation. It also gives rise to an interpretive key of the human experience viewed through the lens of the Christ.

It is important to point out, for purposes of this book and exploration of the Correlation Method, which we will explore in Part 2, that Dr. Jones went on to offer some prophetic prolegomena, which serve as a basis for the submission of the sermon. Kerygmatic content is composed of two factors: the indicative and the imperative. However, it is not just kerygma but the perspective from which the kerygma comes. Dr. Jones was unashamed and unapologetic about his particular perspective as a Black person in the United States. As such, in his teaching, he ushered and nurtured students into connecting the kerygmatic perspective through not only the lens of the life, death, and resurrection of the Christ, but also through the experience of Black people in America and, the Diaspora. It is through the particularity of this hermeneutical lens that Dr. Jones lived, preached, and taught. This is why it is important to be clear on the particularity of the Christ of which we speak and it is from this context I present the correlation model of prophetic preaching.

For centuries the identity of the Christ has been turned into an idol appropriated by white western evangelical theology masking itself as Christianity. Such an idea has infected many in a manner that has been at the root of racism, been used to plunder, and approve of discrimination based on heteronormative categories. In other words, the Christ has been turned into, and taught as, a white supremacist Jesus that justifies and valorizes the sub-human treatment of anything and anyone not deemed as white. This is not just in personal relationships, but in the ways policies are pushed and promoted as well.

However, this is not the case for me and for the Christ of which I speak. When I speak of Christ, I speak of the anointed one born of a teenaged Northeast African unwed mother, who was raised in a town where nothing was known to be good, subjected to all of the lived experiences of one whose town was occupied by paramilitary forces (known as pigs), and murdered by the state for insurrection against the occupying forces of his land. When I speak of the Christ, I speak of the anointed one, who gathered a band of followers to travel the lands doing charity and promoting justice, thereby treating the "people's needs as holy,"[3] while simultaneously challenging the occupying government on its policies, especially against the most vulnerable. When I speak of Christ, I speak of the one who didn't come to die, but to show us how to live. A theology that only celebrates death as one's purpose for existence is a slave theology and is only in service of the manipulation and exploitation of oppressed people and of brown and Black bodies for the benefit of empire. This is not helpful for the scores of oppressed people the world over who, in the words of Howard Thurman in *Jesus and The Disinherited*,[4] have their backs up against the wall.[5] Jesus doesn't come to die, but to show us how to live. And in living, He showed us that sometimes, the ultimate expression of living as your most authentic self may result in death! However, when we speak of the Christ, we are also speaking of the one over whom death did not have the last word due to the power of the resurrection given by the Almighty creator!

This Christ is the Christ commensurate with the Black experience, and the lenses through which we look when interpreting the reality of Jesus. In the words of Dr. Jones, "Jesus is an interpretive reality in need of interpretation." Dr. Jones rebuked placing himself, or our people, in traditional categories crafted by those who had no idea of the Black experience. The particularity of the existence and experience of the Christ was interwoven and interlocked with the particular experience and existence of African-derived people. As such, when looking at the kerygma through an unashamed and unapologetic lens that authenticates this common experience, that which comes forth from the pages and passages of the Bible expresses the word of God for the people of God.

Kerygma is comprised of two components: the indicative and the imperative.

INDICATIVE

The indicative content of kerygmatic content in Christian preaching is the life, death, and resurrection of Jesus Christ. In other words, the indicative means that we interpret life, death, and resurrection through the lenses of the Christ event. Indicative means that there is a special significance behind what you see. In other words, what you see may stand for something deeper than what is seen on the surface. Therefore, when we look at the life, death, and resurrection of Jesus, we must delve into the depths to discover what this means.

LIFE

Life is an interpretive reality. When looking at the life of Jesus, we interpret him as an: authentic being, existing under conditions that seek to negate life for no other reason than the fact that they are who they are!

Looking at Jesus' life as a paradigmatic model, we can see how this applies. He existed under conditions that wanted to negate his life for no substantial reason. While Jesus was yet in the womb, his parents were denied housing. When Jesus was born, a king sought to kill him for no other reason than the fact that he was who he was. While he was living, authorities sought to take Jesus' life simply because he was operating in his own authenticity. He dared to be true to himself, the ancestors from whom he had come, and the God who created him. Because of his efforts to be authentic to who God created him to be, external forces sought to negate his life and existence (and some still do seek to negate his existence). Therefore, life, when seen through the lenses of Jesus' life, is when you can be nothing other than what God created you to be. Because you take this stand, life also says that there will be those who seek to negate your life.

This battle of existence in life is illustrated in current day by the movement for Black lives. Screams and affirmations of Black Lives Matter signify that people want and are demanding the need to simply be themselves in a world and society that would seek to negate our lives. By being authentically who they were created, Black people are targeted and live within conditions that want to negate their being unless they can assimilate and become something "other" than their authentic selves.

DEATH

Death is also an interpretive reality. Death, when seen through the context of Jesus, is not just the cessation of life. Death isn't sickness that terminates life. Death is the curtailment of life at the hands of those who negate your being. Death means to be put to death. In other words, it is life being brought to a close and end by those who would seek to negate one's life simply because they are who they are. We will never know what a forty-year-old Jesus would have done. This is because he was put to death by those who would end his existence simply because he be who he be.

Certainly, we also can identify with this interpretation of life in the days and times in which we live. Numerous humans who have been turned to hashtags exemplify this fact. Whether because of skin being seen as a sin, or corrupt policing, or chaotic communities, or homophobic/transphobic murders, we are too well aware of the curtailment of life at the hands of another who singly sought to negate someone's being because of their authentic existence. Therefore, as an interpretive reality, we are aware of the vices that are systemically and personally placed on people to curtail their existence through sinister acts of evil and present these realities in prophetic preaching. Death may look like cages at the border that have caused families to be separated forever, or women who are forcefully sterilized at the border, or drugs infused into communities—all intended to curtail life. These are pieces of evidence of the acts of negation against a people both individually and collectively that can be interpreted as death.

RESURRECTION

Resurrection, too, is an interpretive reality. Resurrection is being that ought not to be. Being on the other side of having not been. Being that has no business being but that is anyhow. Resurrection means that we exist on the other side of the attacks and attempts to make us not be, or exist. When we look through the eyes of the Christ, we are aware that given all to which he had been subjected, all accounts suggest that he should not have been. All efforts to negate his existence, and curtail his life, should have ensured that he stayed dead. However, resurrection reveals that when one is resurrected, death is negated. Resurrection reveals that there is the possibility of being on the other side of having not been! Resurrection reveals that indeed God has the last word, not those who have sought to negate the very existence of one. It is important to note that, when seriously considered, resurrection does not just mean that Jesus got up from the dead, but Jesus was raised from the dead by the power of God.

When interpreted in our times, we can affirm, as so eloquently offered by Dr. Jones, that people of African descent are a resurrection people. We, among others, are beings who ought not be, given all to which we've been subjected. For a people who have been subjected to evil and exile, experiments and exclusion, plantations and prisons, and all manner of destructive deeds, we should not be here. However, the alternative reality reveals that we are here as a resurrection people. The same can be said for persons reading this book or knowing of someone reading this book who are now resurrected from some deadly predicament. Resurrection is being that ought not be, and should be celebrated as such, as a people raised from the dead by the power of God.

IMPERATIVE

After considering the indicative component of kerygmatic fulfillment, the next movement is the imperative. The imperative is the response. Once the indicative is heard, there is some action that must take place as a result of hearing the indicative. The imperative is done based on what is heard in the indicative. The imperative is about the lifestyle of transformation that comes as a result of hearing the indicative. In other words, what should be done as a result of hearing the indicative? What shall we do now, as a result of hearing what we have heard? What is the proclamation calling the people to do as a result of hearing the imperative?

It is this imperative to which the indicative points and moves the listener. Particularly in prophetic preaching, this indicative must be made clear as an alternative reality is proposed. While the indicative will be referred to in part 2, the imperative will be the central theme of part 3 as we look to movement.

CONCLUSION

In this chapter, we have explored some of the foundational prolegomena essential to Dr. Jones for the Correlation Method of preaching. We have explored the definition of a sermon, as well as the particularity of the hermeneutical lens essential to utilize the Correlation Method. Take special note that the kerygmatic foundation offered by Dr. Jones was also centered on connecting the Christ with the Black experience. Ultimately, out of this indicative of life, death, and resurrection should come the imperative. The imperative is the call to transformation as a result of hearing the indicative.

With these foundational elements in place, we now move to the Correlation Method.

QUESTIONS TO CONSIDER

1. What is the definition of a sermon?
2. Explain the three components of a sermon.
3. How does the definition of a sermon connect to the approaches to a sermon found in Chapter 2?
4. What is kerygma?
5. What are the components of kerygma?
6. What are the components of the indicative?
7. What is the imperative?

NOTES

1. Jones, Miles Jerome, "The Sermon as A Submitted Statement" in *Born To Preach: Essays in Honor of The Ministry of Henry & Ella Mitchell*, edited by Samuel K. Roberts (Valley Forge, PA: Judson Press, 2000), 62.

2. See https://www.pbs.org/wnet/religionandethics/2002/05/03/may-3-2002-robert-franklin-extended-interview/11657/, accessed March 9, 2021.

3. Obery Hendricks, *The Politics of Jesus: Rediscovering the True Revolutionary Nature of the Teachings of Jesus and how They Have Been Corrupted* (New York: Doubleday, 2006).

4. Howard Thurman, *Jesus and the Disinherited* (Boston: Beacon Press, 1976.

5. In Howard Thurman's book titled *Jesus and the Disinherited*, Thurman investigates and inquiries about the significance of the religion of Jesus to those with "their backs against the wall."

METHOD

METHOD

Neither time nor space will permit a thorough excavation and examination of the meaning and ministry of Dr. Miles Jerome Jones as pastor, professor, public servant, and person. The man, his ministry, and what he means to the worlds of academia, church, and community demand scholarly study. Dr. Jones lived by the motto believed to be offered by St. Francis of Assisi, "Preach the gospel at all times. When necessary, use words." Dr. Jones' focus on the importance of authenticity in sermonic definition, and experiential application was a key component of his consciousness, and the call to which he was faithful. His concern was for life to be experienced and not categorized or placed in a box, and that concern extended beyond his life. This is why he had his papers destroyed so that he would not be categorized, even by friends. Dr. Jones did not want to be interpreted through papers but wanted his being to inform those who would attempt to experience him. This deep dive forces those who loved and learned from Dr. Jones to share him through the experience of who he was.

I share this brief reflection of Dr. Jones to provide a baseline example for understanding the method he taught to countless students. The method is called the Correlation Method of Preaching. The chapters in this part of the book will walk you through each of the components of the method as you construct a sermon. Of particular importance is the definition of a sermon as utilized by Dr. Jones. It is this definition that is especially relevant to the approaches and definitions found in Part 1 of this book.

As a brief introduction, the Correlation Method links the scripture selected for preaching to a particular situation at hand. This linkage, which lifts and locks together the scripture and situation, gives birth to what is called an organizing observation. The organizing observation sets the framework for the entire sermon. Out of this organizing observation flows the structure of the sermon. The structure includes the title, which is not only what the sermon is called, but what the entire sermon is about. Next is the introduction, which acquaints the listener to the text and narrows the generality of the situation at hand to the specificity of the linkage of how this selected scriptural text addresses the aforementioned situation at hand. This is followed by the body of the sermon, and the closing and fulfillment of the sermon.

The structure of the sermon is the Correlation Method. However, as important, if not more important to the structure of the sermon, is the substance of the sermon. The substance of the sermon should reflect the work of prayer, study, and reflection of the preacher. The importance of the work that produces the substance of the sermon cannot be overstated. Structure is important. Substance is important. Even more important is the substance of the preacher. As has been stated, the structure is how the sermon is put together. The authentic, or as Thurman would say, "the sound of the genuine" in you is how you are put together. How you are put together ought to inform how the sermon and substance thereof are projected in the proclamation. In the pages that follow, you will find the structure. However, keep in mind structure means nothing without substance. So, let's move into this method of prophetic preaching, not forgetting the meaning of the same.

CHAPTER 4

ORGANIZING OBSERVATION & TITLE

The Correlation Method is the process of linking the scripture selected with the situation at hand discerned in the selected scripture. That is, each passage of scripture has within it a certain condition of existence. This is why it is important to spend time with and dig into the scripture selected, and not attempt to proof text one scripture with another. Proof texting means trying to prove or validate one scripture by using another scripture that may or may not be taken from a similar context. Each of the scriptures was written at a certain time and place with a context possibly different than other scriptures. Therefore, the work of the preacher is to correlate the scripture with the situation at hand. Readers should note that condition of existence and the situation at hand will be used interchangeably!

It is the preacher's task to discern this condition of existence and develop how this condition is addressed through this scripture. In other words, how does this scriptural text address the condition of existence at hand?

ORGANIZING OBSERVATION

In the discipline of architecture, the cornerstone is the first stone laid around which all other stones will be built. The cornerstone serves as the reference point for the purposed placement of all other stones used to erect the edifice. It is no wonder why Jesus' quoting of Psalm 118:22 that "the stone that the builders rejected has now become the chief cornerstone" (Matthew 21:42) is such a powerful metaphorical message. The very one who was thrown away and treated as trash has now become the one around whom a movement is built!

The cornerstone, again, is the reference point against which all other stones receive their orientation. The organizing observation is the cornerstone around which the sermon is crafted and constructed. In the Correlation Method, the entire sermon ought to point to the organizing observation. If the substance of the sermon does not point back to the organizing observation, then it is to be reserved for another sermon. The importance of discerning the organizing observation cannot be overstated.

The organizing observation is an essential component of the sermon construction process. The organizing observation is what the entire sermon will have said in two sentences. The organizing observation (OO) is a test of the preacher's ability to discern the connectedness of the scripture and situation, and the ability to express the connectedness the preacher has discerned. The OO requires the preacher to ask and answer two questions: (1) What is the condition of existence made evident by this text? and (2) In what way does this text address this condition?

It is important to note here that the discerning of the condition of existence is the concerning of one condition of existence. A Scripture may have more than one condition of existence. If so, then there is more than one sermon that may come from that scripture. However, for purposes of this method, it is important to discern one condition of existence and dig into that one condition of existence!

It cannot be stated enough that the organizing observation is the cornerstone of the sermon. After the questions have been answered above, the organizing observation is crafted as the entire sermon in two sentences. These two sentences begin with the phrases that follow:

There are times when . . .
When such occurs . . .

The time of sitting with God in prayer, meditation, study, and other practices as a part of the preparation for preaching is seminal to sermonic construction. This time of sitting and listening gives insight through the connection with the Creator as to what God would have us to lift as a lesson from the passage. Sitting with the scripture, the Creator, and the ancestors until you have discerned that this is the message the Divine has called you to deliver is of utmost importance.

The sentence, "There are times when . . ." should relay the condition of existence discerned by sitting with God and the scripture selected, based on the lenses of yourself, your study of the context of scripture, and the view of society discussed in Chapter 2. In this way you are bringing your own sacred text to the sacred text, in the discerning of the condition of existence.

The sentence, "When such occurs . . ." should reveal how, through prayer, the labor of study, and the lenses of your own sacred story, you have discerned how this text addresses the condition of existence expressed in the first sentence.

These two sentences comprise the organizing observation, which is your entire sermon in two sentences.

Let us look at a passage as an example. Throughout the remainder of Part 2, we will walk through this passage together to demonstrate, from start to finish, the method.

EXODUS 1:15-22, NRSV

[15]The king of Egypt said to the Hebrew midwives, one of whom was named Shiphrah and the other Puah, [16]"When you act as midwives to the Hebrew women, and see them on the birthstool, if it is a boy, kill him; but if it is a girl, she shall live." [17]But the midwives feared God; they did not do as the king of Egypt commanded them, but they let the boys live. [18]So the king of Egypt summoned the midwives and said to them, "Why have you done this, and allowed the boys to live?" [19]The midwives said to Pharaoh, "Because the Hebrew women are not like the Egyptian women; for they are vigorous and give birth before the midwife comes to them." [20]So God dealt well with the midwives; and the people multiplied and became very strong. [21]And because the midwives feared God, he gave them families. [22]Then Pharaoh commanded all his people, "Every boy that is born to the Hebrews you shall throw into the Nile, but you shall let every girl live."

ORGANIZING OBSERVATION

There are times when . . . *violence visits the vicinities of the vulnerable.*

When such occurs . . . *this text teaches us how to proceed in partnership with God to gain victory over violence.*

In the passage selected above, the general condition of existence discerned by the preacher is a condition of violence. The violence discerned is initiated by the state against the most vulnerable of society. The violence discerned comes by way of policies that dictate to workers and laborers that mothers in the vulnerable position of giving birth must throw away the children they have been carrying in their womb for months. This is not only violence against the children, but violence against the mothers and other relatives of the children. The condition of existence is one of violence.

In the second sentence, the preacher has discerned that the way this text addresses this violence is by showing that proceeding in partnership with God will gain victory over the violence in the land.

These two sentences form the organizing observation for the entire sermon. When the entire sermon is completed, the preacher will have said what the sentences have submitted. The clarity of this cornerstone is an important part of the entire sermon construction process because this keeps the preacher on task for this sermon. In other words, the entire sermon should point to this condition of existence and how this scripture is addressing this condition of existence. With this in mind, we now move toward the selection of a title.

TITLE

"If you don't name right, you won't aim right,"[1] suggests Dr. Katie Canon regarding the importance of giving the sermon the proper title. The title of the sermon is the label that is placed on the lesson. The title of the sermon is not only what you call it but what the entire sermon is about. The title of the sermon is the sum total of the entire sermon. In the words of Dr. Jones, the sermon's title should be a "short, pithy statement that reveals the distilled essence" of the substance of the sermon.

I can remember my grandmother buying orange juice in frozen tin cans of concentrate. These cans of concentrate were then placed in a pitcher. Grandma would have to add water to the concentrate to make the orange juice in the pitcher for all to enjoy. The title of the sermon is the concentrate, or distilled essence of the sermon. The remainder of the sermon will be akin to the water that is added for all to enjoy.

There are different ways to get to a title. Some may come through readings, musings, music, or other means. Be open and creative with titles. It is important to note, however, that a title should not be given to a sermon out of a desire to be popular or engage in simple shock value. If the title that emanates from the sermon happens to be popular or filled with shock value, then so be it. However, selecting a title simply because it sounds good or creates shock or is a popular poem, song, or saying diminishes the integrity of the sermon. Remember, the title is the distilled essence of the sermon. It is important to allow the sermon to give you the title and not let the title make the sermon. It is dangerous to get the title before you get the sermon or the organizing observation.

Doing so may steer the hearer and possibly the preacher in a direction that the text and or sermon is not organically or authentically meant to go. Again, this is why it is vitally important to name right so that you can aim right. And if the preacher chooses to use a question as a title, then the sermon should answer the question.

EXODUS 1:15-22

[15]The king of Egypt said to the Hebrew midwives, one of whom was named Shiphrah and the other Puah, [16]"When you act as midwives to the Hebrew women, and see them on the birthstool, if it is a boy, kill him; but if it is a girl, she shall live." [17]But the midwives feared God; they did not do as the king of Egypt commanded them, but they let the boys live. [18]So the king of Egypt summoned the midwives and said to them, "Why have you done this, and allowed the boys to live?" [19]The midwives said to Pharaoh, "Because the Hebrew women are not like the Egyptian women; for they are vigorous and give birth before the midwife comes to them." [20]So God dealt well with the midwives; and the people multiplied and became very strong. [21]And because the midwives feared God, he gave them families. [22]Then Pharaoh commanded all his people, "Every boy that is born to the Hebrews you shall throw into the Nile, but you shall let every girl live."[2]

ORGANIZING OBSERVATION

There are times when . . . *violence visits the vicinities of the vulnerable.*

When such occurs . . . *this text teaches us how to proceed in partnership with God to gain victory over violence.*

Title: Victory Over Violence

QUESTIONS TO CONSIDER

1. What is the organizing observation?
2. What are the two sentences that comprise the organizing observation?
3. What is the title?
4. What are the considerations for a good title?

NOTES

1. This statement is taken from a lecture given by Katie G. Canon in the class Social Teachings in Sacred Rhetoric in January 2002 at Union Presbyterian Theological School in Richmond, Virginia.

2. Exodus 1:15-22 from *The HarperCollins Study Bible* (New York: HarperCollins, 2006).

CHAPTER 5

INTRODUCTION & TRANSITION

*The introduction acquaints, to get
the attention of the listener.*
—MILES JONES

INTRODUCTION

On October 3, 1887, with two professors and fifteen students, an academic institution was founded and named the State Normal College for Colored Students. "In 1891, the College received $7,500 under the Second Morrill Act for agricultural and mechanical arts education, and the State Normal College for Colored Students became Florida's land grant institution for colored people. At about this time, the College was relocated from its original site on Copeland Street to its present location, and its name was changed to the State Normal and Industrial College for Colored Students."[1] The land granted to the State Normal Industrial College for Colored Students, was granted because it was some of the worst land in the city, as it was infested with rattlesnakes. The "gift" of this bad land to this new institution indicated that the students were counted out even at its inception. The same institution which was "gifted" this bad land is now the Florida Agricultural & Mechanical University. Florida A&M University, is now one of the best institutions of higher learning in the country, named in recent years as the top public historically Black college and university by *U.S. News and World Report* in 2019. I am also a proud alum of Florida A&M.

In the School of Business and Industry at Florida A&M, under the leadership of Dean Sybil C. Mobley, students were blessed to interact weekly with executives of Fortune-500 companies through receptions and schoolwide forums. As part of our engagement with these executives, we were given a formula for introducing ourselves prior to asking our questions. The introductory formula required that we give our name, our major, and the city from which we hailed. The introduction was important because it gave the hearer just enough about us prior to receiving the rest of what we had to offer in the way of a question.

In like manner, the sermon's introduction is intended to give the hearer just enough about the subject and sermonic theme to arrest their attention prior to going deeper into the sermon. A good introduction will cause the listener to be pained if they do not get to hear the rest of the matter to which they are being introduced.

It is helpful to think of an introduction as we would the porch of a house. Those who know the housing market know the value of having curb appeal. Curb appeal is the aesthetic given to the exterior of a house, which causes one to want to explore what is in the interior. Metaphorically speaking, as a porch, the introduction of the sermon is designed to attract you and lead you into the house of the sermon.

Good porches are inviting and enchanting with good curb appeal, if you will. Good porches are not cumbered with clutter but capture your consciousness and curiosity to the extent that you desire to experience the inside of the house. In other words, furniture meant for the inside of the house ought not be placed on the porch. Think about how you would feel if invited to a home, where the bathroom sink, shower, and washing machine were all on the porch prior to your entry. What would you think if you found the pantry, sofas, and entertainment centers all on the porch? If all of these items were on the porch, it would likely discourage one from the desire to enter the home and explore what is inside. The same is to be said about a good introduction to a sermon. Treat the introduction like a good porch; make it inviting but not extensive. Good introductions are lean and not too long and garner your attention with good curb appeal.

We now turn our attention to the construction of a good introduction. The introduction's purpose is to acquaint the listener with the text. The introduction is that which leads me from the generality of the outside to the specificity of the inside. It is leading the hearer on a journey. It gets the attention of the hearer and makes them want to hear more. It has been said that if a listener's attention is not arrested in the first five minutes of the sermon, their attention will be gone for good. The introduction should assist the listener by being very clear as to what you have in mind. As the introduction proceeds, it will move from the general condition of existence to the specificity of the passage.

This is where we begin to employ the organizing observation. The introduction moves us from generality to the specificity of how this text addresses the condition of existence we have discerned. This general condition of existence may be expressed in many ways. Some choose to use sermon illustrations. Sermon illustrations, or stories, life experiences, poems, song lyrics, quotes, and current events can be great ways to connect with people in the introduction, as long as the aforementioned examples are grounded in and connected to moving from the generality of the condition of existence to the specificity of how this text will address said condition. It is up to the preacher to work with how they will identify the condition of existence.

The point to be remembered is that addressing this condition of existence in the introduction will also require that this general condition of existence somehow move to the specificity of how this scripture will address said condition of existence. The illustration below emphasizes this point.

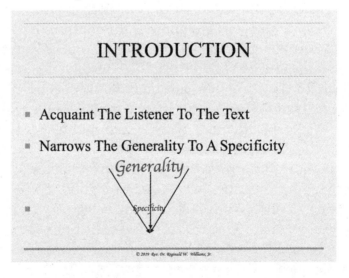

Let us look back at the sermon we've begun to construct for the introduction.

EXODUS 1:15-22

¹⁵The king of Egypt said to the Hebrew midwives, one of whom was named Shiphrah and the other Puah, ¹⁶"When you act as midwives to the Hebrew women, and see them on the birthstool, if it is a boy, kill him; but if it is a girl, she shall live." ¹⁷But the midwives feared God; they did not do as the king of Egypt commanded them, but they let the boys live. ¹⁸So the king of Egypt summoned the midwives and said to them, "Why have you done this, and allowed the boys to live?" ¹⁹The midwives said to Pharaoh, "Because the Hebrew women are not like the Egyptian women; for they are vigorous and give birth before the midwife comes to them." ²⁰So God dealt well with the midwives; and the people multiplied and became very strong. ²¹And because the midwives feared God, he gave them families. ²²Then Pharaoh commanded all his people, "Every boy that is born to the Hebrews you shall throw into the Nile, but you shall let every girl live."[2]

ORGANIZING OBSERVATION

There are times when . . . *violence visits the vicinities of the vulnerable.*

When such occurs . . . *this text teaches us how to proceed in partnership with God to gain victory over violence.*

Title: Victory Over Violence

Intro: *In 1971, Marvin Gaye wrote a song that was part of an album with the same title as the song. And in that song, he asked a very important question. When he looked around and saw how war was killing innocent people. When he looked around and saw how racism was violating his own people. When he saw how people could fight for their country, then come home and be treated like trash by the same country they fought for, Marvin asked this question, "What's Going On?" Marvin asked a question in order to gain some understanding, because he realized that there are times when violence is the unwelcome visitor that visits the vulnerable. We know something about that right here in Chicago, don't we? When we look and see how it is easier to get a gun than it is a loaf of bread in a food desert, we can attest to the fact that violence visits our vicinities. When such occurs, however, the text shows us that we can partner with God to gain victory over violence.*

In this introduction, we see the general condition of existence being that of a context of violence. This condition of existence is connected and communicated through a song known to many in the congregation, and conditions in the communities in which members of the congregation live. The introduction further suggests that this scripture text addresses the condition of violence by showing us how we can gain victory over violence. In other words, that is how the generality of violence is met with the specificity of this passage. Notice also that the organizing observation is utilized in the introduction. The organizing observation helps to guide the introduction from generality to how this passage will specifically address said generality. What comes next is the transition.

TRANSITION

The transition of the sermon is a critical and key component of the sermon. The transition is the portal through which the hearer passes to get from the porch into the house, and the critical door that moves us into the main part of the sermon.

This door may be fashioned in a few ways. One way to transition is to simply invite the listener on the journey and beckon them to come into the house. This is a simple invitation asking the listener to follow you as you lead them into the house of the sermon in order to show them around as a good host should. A sentence as simple as, "Come with me as we explore how this scripture teaches us . . ." provides ample invitation. The importance of the transition aids the listener in understanding that you are on a journey together.

Another way to transition into the house of the sermon is to use a question, sometimes called a relevant question. That is, on the heels of your introduction, what is the most relevant question that can be asked as a result of hearing the introduction that will lead us into the house of the sermon. Adherents to the Dialectical Method offered by Samuel Dewitt Proctor in his classic opus *The Certain Sound of The Trumpet* [3] will recognize this language and terminology from that method. In that method, the relevant question comes as a result of the tension that emanates from the thesis and antithesis. While the method is different, the purpose of the question is similar. That is, the purpose of the question is to invite the hearer on the journey through the door of the question to get the answer to the question that has been asked. It goes without saying that if you use the question as a door, then the sermon must answer the question.

These transitory question or statement helps the listener to journey into the house of the sermon. Let's take the sermon we are constructing as an example.

ORGANIZING OBSERVATION

There are times when . . . *violence visits the vicinities in which we live.*

When such occurs . . . *this text teaches us how to proceed in partnership with God to gain victory over violence.*

Title: Victory Over Violence

Intro: *In 1971, Marvin Gaye wrote a song that was part of an album with the same title as the song. And in that song, he asked a very important question. When he looked around and saw how war was killing innocent people. When he looked around and saw how racism was violating his own people. When he saw how people could fight for their country, then come home and be treated like trash by the same country they fought for, Marvin asked this question, "What's Going On?" Marvin asked a question in order to gain some understanding, because he realized that there are times when violence is the unwelcome visitor that visits the vulnerable. We know something about that right here in Chicago, don't we? When we look and see how it is easier to get a gun than it is a loaf of bread in a food desert, we can attest to the fact that violence visits our vicinities. When such occurs, however, the text shows us that we can partner with God to gain victory over violence.*

TRANSITION

Transition: *Come with me, and let's see how the text shows us how we can gain victory over violence.*

or

RQ: *Well, the question is: How can we gain victory over violence?*

Either one of these transitory tools will lead us from the porch of the sermon into the house of the sermon to invite the listener on a journey to discover how we can gain victory over violence. It is important to note that the transition statement or the relevant question invites the hearer into the sermon by referring the question or invitation back to the second sentence of the organizing observation. In other words, in the sermon above, both the statement and the question invite or ask how we can gain victory over violence. This keeps the integrity of the sermon intact so that a question or invitation is not asked that leads the sermon in an unintended direction. There is no need to use both transition statements and relevant questions. Selecting one of these transitory tools will suffice in the effort to lead the listener into the house of the sermon.

QUESTIONS TO CONSIDER

1. What is an introduction?
2. What is the purpose of the introduction?
3. To what shall we liken the introduction?
4. What is the purpose of the transition?
5. What are two ways we can transition into the house of the sermon?

NOTES

1. See https://www.famu.edu/index.cfm?AboutFAMU&History, accessed on April 28, 2021.

2. Exodus 1:15-22 from *The HarperCollins Study Bible* (New York: HarperCollins, 2006).

3. Samuel D. Proctor, *The Certain Sound of the Trumpet: Crafting a Sermon of Authority* (Valley Forge, PA: Judson Press, 1994).

CHAPTER 6

MOVES / POINTS

*Don't develop so much in the introduction that
there's nothing left for the body.*
—MILES JONES (OCTOBER 6, 1999)

We now turn our attention to the body of the sermon. If the introduction is the porch, the body of the sermon is the house. Prayerfully, the curb appeal of the introduction has invited the hearer to want to know what's inside of the house, known as the body of the sermon. In other words, if the introduction is the appetizer, the body of the sermon is the main course of a meal. It is the body of the sermon that the people are waiting to hear and for which they came to be fed. The body of the sermon is that to which the introduction and transition point. So hopefully, the listener has been enticed by the porch, and invited through the door, and is now ready to enter the house of the sermon. It is in the house of the sermon where we move from the surface to the substance that has been discerned by the preacher.

In this book, I offer a way to express the body of the sermon through what is known as moves or points.

Please remember this is one way, not the only way. Some preachers prefer not to use points, and that is fine. Points, however, may assist the listener as a pedagogical tool, in remembering and internalizing the sermon for the journey ahead.

As an example, I remember one sermon from over twenty years ago, preached by my pastor, the Rev. Dr. Jeremiah A. Wright, Jr. It is the sermon on which I accepted my call to ministry. On the first Sunday in Advent 1998, Pastor Wright preached a sermon titled, "When God Disrupts Your Agenda" from Luke 1. His focus was on Zechariah's agenda of performing the duties of the priest being disrupted by the angel of the Lord. While I may not remember all of the sermon, I do remember the points. Pastor Wright proclaimed that when God disrupts your agenda, there will be: 1) unsettling doubt, 2) unrelenting fear, and 3) God's unfailing promise. The alliteration offered also helps with the ability to remember the sermon points/moves.

In discerning the points of the sermon, the preacher should remember that the points discerned must flow out of the sermon. In other words, when you transition into the house by inviting the hearer to come with you, make sure that you are leading them into the intended house and not another house. The points you make should be intentional and directly related to the purpose and point of the sermon. If you are inviting the hearer into the house using a question, make sure that the body of the sermon is answering the question asked.

There is nothing worse than to have the body of a sermon disjointed from the introduction and title of the sermon. This is why it is important to do the very important work at the beginning of the sermon of crafting the organizing observation as expressed in Chapter 4.

The organizing observation is the central piece of the sermon. Everything in the body of the sermon should seamlessly flow out of and lead back to that organizing observation. The points of the sermon should flow directly from the introduction and the transition into the body of the sermon.

As an example, let's look at the sermon we have been working with heretofore.

ORGANIZING OBSERVATION

There are times when . . . *violence visits the vicinities in which we live.*

When such occurs . . . *this text teaches us how to proceed in partnership with God to gain victory over violence.*

Title: Victory Over Violence

Intro: *In 1971, Marvin Gaye wrote a song that was part of an album with the same title as the song. And in that song, he asked a very important question. When he looked around and saw how war was killing innocent people. When he looked around and saw how racism was violating his own people. When he saw how people could fight for their country, then come home and be treated like trash by the same country they fought for, Marvin asked this question, "What's Going On?" Marvin asked a question in order to gain some understanding, because he realized that there are times when violence is the unwelcome visitor that visits the vulnerable. We know something about that right here in Chicago, don't we? When we look and see how it is easier to get a gun than it is a loaf of bread in a food desert, we can attest to the fact that violence visits our vicinities. When such occurs, however, the text shows us that we can partner with God to gain victory over violence.*

Transition: *Come with me, and let's see how the text shows us how we can gain victory over violence.*

or

RQ: *Well, the question is: How can we gain victory over violence?*

With this introduction and transition, the body of the sermon should either answer the question, or show us how the scripture instructs us how to have victory over violence. Again, the structure of constructing a point offered is a way, not the only way. It should be noted that this is not necessarily part of the Correlation Method as taught by Dr. Jones but is offered here as a resource for preachers.

POINT DISCERNMENT

The development of points should come after the points have been discerned. The discerning of the points comes as we explore either what we are showing to the hearer as we invite them into the house or answering the question that is asked in the transition. We discern the points through careful exploration of the passage, sitting with the text, exploring the scripture, thinking about the condition of the people to whom we are preaching, and sitting with the Creator to hear and be led in our efforts.

Let's look at the sermon we are exploring.

ORGANIZING OBSERVATION

There are times when . . . *violence visits the vicinities in which we live.*

When such occurs . . . *the text shows us how to proceed in partnership with God to gain victory over violence.*

Title: Victory Over Violence

Intro: *In 1971, Marvin Gaye wrote a song that was part of an album with the same title as the song. And in that song, he asked a very important question. When he looked around and saw how war was killing innocent people. When he looked around and saw how racism was violating his own people. When he saw how people could fight for their country, then come home and be treated like trash by the same country they fought for, Marvin asked this question, "What's Going On?" Marvin asked a question in order to gain some understanding, because he realized that there are times when violence is the unwelcome visitor that visits the vulnerable. We know something about that right here in Chicago, don't we? When we look and see how it is easier to get a gun than it is a loaf of bread in a food desert, we can attest to the fact that violence visits our vicinities. When such occurs, however, the text shows us that we can partner with God to gain victory over violence.*

Transition: *Come with me, and let's see how the text shows us how we can gain victory over violence.*

or

RQ: *Well, the question is: How can we gain victory over violence?*

BODY

1. Attitude of Reverence
2. Acts of Resistance
3. Acceptance of Redemption

In the example above, the preacher has discerned that the invitation into the house will show that victory can be gained over violence through an Attitude of Resistance, Acts of Resistance, and the Acceptance of Redemption. These are the three points the preacher has discerned, which flow out of the introduction and transition based on the organizing observation. The work to be done now is to develop each of these points. To this, we now turn.

POINT DEVELOPMENT

When developing a point, it is important to name the point. When naming the point, the same rules apply as with giving a title to the sermon. The preacher must make sure to state what this point is as it relates to the entire sermon. In illustrating the point, I offer a way to develop this fully. This was taught to me by Nathan Quick, another one of Dr. Jones' students. Each point can be developed by remembering the acronym IEIA. This stands for Image, Explanation, Illustration, Application. Let's go through each.

IMAGE

The first component of point development is painting the image of the point as it relates to the text. In other words, the image is to help the people see what you are saying. Here is where the preacher engages the five senses and transports the hearer into the world where they can experience what is being expressed. Here is where it is incumbent on the preacher to be conversant with a viable vocabulary. In the words of Dr. Jones, "Words are our stock and trade." This simply means that in order to connect with the congregation and link with the listener, the preacher must employ the vocabulary to literally paint the picture of the point. Preachers must be readers. The reading of poetry and prose will aid and assist the preacher in accessing vocabulary of imagery.

EXPLANATION

The explanation of the point aids the listener in understanding any contextual clues or missed meanings that may be hidden beneath the surface of the scripture. It is here where the preacher includes any exegesis, word study, hidden meanings, euphemisms, etc., that may not be apparent to the naked eye. This is where the preacher expresses the fruit of their homework, as it relates to this point. It should be noted that it is not necessary to preach all of one's exegesis. However, if there are special matters that give meaning and understanding as it relates to the point, this is the place to include that information.

ILLUSTRATION

Illustrations are vignettes, pictures, stories, common experiences, etc., that assist the hearers in seeing what the preacher is saying in order to drive the point home. The power of stories is that stories allow the listeners to place themselves in the story or apply the story to their own predicament. In doing so, stories assist and aid in understanding what the preacher is saying. Dr. Jones pressed the point about clarifying the difference between illustration and interpretation. Illustration shows you something as it is. The interpretation is what is meant by what is pictured. One can help clarify the other, and both are extremely useful in sermon construction and proclamation.

Preachers who read this would do well to begin to collect a notebook, or file, for different stories. Illustrations illumine the mind and meaning of the preaching that comes forth. Illustrations are not only stories but may be poems, songs, experiences, news clippings, or anything familiar to the listeners that would help the listener understand all the more the point being driven home by the preacher. Care should also be taken not to over-illustrate.

APPLICATION

Application is driving the point home by applying the point to the person. Here is where the point is made real in the person's life. The application of the point is an integral piece of the point as it forces the listener to come face to face with how this point affects her or him. It is here where the preacher should also know their audience as well as possible, so as to make meaningful connections in the application of the point.

Let's see how the point development looks with the sermon we have been working on heretofore.

ORGANIZING OBSERVATION

There are times when . . . *violence visits the vicinities in which we live.*

When such occurs . . . *this text shows us how to proceed in partnership with God to gain victory over violence*

Title: Victory Over Violence

Intro: *In 1971, Marvin Gaye wrote a song that was part of an album with the same title as the song. And in that song, he asked a very important question. When he looked around and saw how war was killing innocent people. When he looked around and saw how racism was violating his own people. When he saw how people could fight for their country, then come home and be treated like trash by the same country they fought for, Marvin asked this question, "What's Going On?" Marvin asked a question in order to gain some understanding, because he realized that there are times when violence is the unwelcome visitor that visits the vulnerable. We* *know something about that right here in Chicago, don't we? When we look and see how it is easier to get a gun than it is a loaf of bread in a food desert, we can attest to the fact that violence visits our vicinities. When such occurs, however, the text shows us that we can partner with God to gain victory over violence.*

TRANSITION

Transition: *Come with me, and let's see how the text shows us how we can gain victory over violence.*

or

RQ: *Well, the question is: How can we gain victory over violence?*

MOVES/POINTS:

- Attitude of Reverence
  - **Image**—The text shows that we can gain victory over violence when we first of all have proper reverence. Can you see the midwives? They have just been called into the office and been informed of the edict that has come across the desk of the head midwife. An edict has been issued that declares that any child born with male genitalia must be killed by the very ones whose hands have helped usher them into the world. Can you feel their pain? These wise and wonderful African women have dedicated their lives to ensuring that life comes in the world safe and sound. These sisters with their sacred work are told by the king to kill the boys but let the girls live. Can you feel their frustration? I mean, this is the king talking. This is the one who

is the ruler over the land. This is the one who is in power. This is the one who is to be respected and revered by the nation. This is the king telling these who help usher life, to undercut life. The king tells them to kill the boys and let the girls live. But, the text goes on to say, the midwives feared God.

- **Explanation**—The midwives feared God. That word arrested my attention because when I did my homework, I discovered that the word for feared in this text does not mean to be afraid of, but in awe of. The word fear really means reverence. They reverenced God because they had a relationship with God. And they knew that God would not have them kill any child. The midwives may have respected the king's position, but the midwives reverenced God's power. The king may have demanded their respect due to his position, but the midwives saved their reverence for God. And so these midwives would not take the life of a child because they reverenced God.

- **Illustration**—The story is told of a pastor who shepherded a congregation on the East Coast. And in this congregation were some of the movers and shakers of that city. One Sunday, the pastor preached a sermon that spoke to God's desire for justice for the poor and dispossessed. In the sermon, the pastor was critical of policies in the city government. Some of the movers and shakers who were part of that city government asked

speak with the pastor after service, and
demanded that the pastor recant the pronouncements in the sermon as it related to
city government. These movers and shakers,
who were also great donors, also threatened
the pastor with withholding their monies if
the pastor didn't recant. The pastor, realizing
that these were people with some power
and paper, stood flat-footed and responded
to the request to recant. The pastor said, "I
have been called by God to preach, not by
politicians to pander. And I could not stand
by and watch the poor and dispossessed that
God loves so much die on the front porches
of this city, while the government continues
to pass policies that plunder the poor. So I
understand that you will do what you have
to do. And I will do what I have to do." And
right there, the pastor may have respected
the movers and shakers. But the pastor gave
reverence to God.

- **Application**—When you reverence God,
  you will remember that it is God who is the
  Creator, not politicians who want you to
  ponder. When you reverence God, you will
  put God in God's proper place. Too often we
  reverence people and put them on pedestals,
  when in fact the reverence belongs to God.
  It wasn't the politicians who opened your
  eyes or blew breath in your body. It wasn't
  the pundits who knew your before you were
  born and gave you a purpose to live out
  in this world. God opened your eyes this

morning. God put breath in your body and the beat in your heart. God gave you the food you eat, and shoes for your feet. As a matter of fact, somewhere I read it was God who made us and not we ourselves. So, while others may or may not get my respect, my reverence belongs to God and God alone! If we want to gain victory over violence, we must first, like these midwives, have proper reverence for God.

You now have the first point for a sermon titled, Victory over Violence.

QUESTIONS TO CONSIDER

1. Must all sermons have points? What is your preference?
2. What is the benefit of having sermon development with points?
3. How can points serve as a pedagogical tool?
4. Describe the four components of developing a point as described in this chapter.

CHAPTER 7

FULFILLING THE SERMON

Requirement of Kerygma must move toward
fulfillment and not just conclusion.
—MILES JONES (SEPTEMBER 16, 1999)

On my iPad, I have an app that takes the pictures stored on my device and converts them into puzzles. The app takes the picture selected, breaks the picture up into pieces and shapes, and challenges me to put the pieces back together in order to show the picture selected. The gift of the application is that in putting the pieces of the puzzle together, we are empowered to begin with the end in mind. We see the big picture in order to put together the small pieces. In like manner, the preacher does not commence the creation of the sermon without having in mind the conclusion of the sermon. The preacher should start with the end, or the big and completed picture, in mind.

The concern of this part of the sermon is not just the conclusion of the sermon but the fulfillment—why the sermon was even preached in the first place. This is the purpose of beginning the sermon construction process with the organizing observation. We have already identified the organizing observation as the cornerstone. Another metaphor to assist in our understanding suggests that just as Harriet Tubman watched the North Star to guide her and her people to freedom, the organizing observation again serves as a North Star to guide us to where we are going. Therefore, in fulfilling the sermon, the test is to ensure that the sermon as concluded fulfills the mission of the organizing observation.

A word should be said here about the difference between conclusion and fulfillment. According to Dr. Jones, the sermon should move toward fulfillment, not just conclusion. Conclusion is just the end of the sermon. Fulfillment is the purpose for which the sermon is realized.

In her book *Doing the Deed*,[1] Martha Simmons offers some practical hints about "celebrating" and concluding a sermon. She offers clear characteristics about celebration and strategies for developing the same. She also gives the difference between celebration and conclusion. This is important because, "a celebration is a conclusion. However not all conclusions are celebrations."[2] One would do well to gain insight into the construction of conclusions and celebrations from *Doing the Deed*, *They Like to Never Quit Praising God*,[3] and other texts that give great attention to the closing, conclusion, and celebration of the sermon.

My focus, however, is not just on the conclusion of the sermon, but the fulfillment of the sermon. Conclusion is only the end. Fulfillment is the end for which the idea was ever conceived. Focus on fulfillment is warranted so that we are not guilty of concluding and celebrating a sermon without the sermon's purpose ever being fulfilled. A sermon's fulfillment means that the sermon accomplishes what it was conceived to accomplish.

Consider the classroom example given by Dr. Jones of a water glass. The purpose of the water glass is to hold liquid. This purpose is fully realized when the glass is filled to capacity. The full purpose of the glass is realized when the glass holds all that it is able to hold. When the glass is full because it is totally filled, then it is fulfilled. When it is fully filled, then its purpose is fully realized. Now whether in person or in sermon, one can choose to live in a way that indicates that the glass is half full. But a person or sermon that is halfway is not realizing its full purpose.

With the notion of fulfillment, it is important to note that the fulfillment of the sermon, according to the Correlation Method taught by Dr. Jones, must also fulfill the kerygmatic thrust of the sermon. Remember that kerygma, as explained in Chapter 2, is the interpretation of the life, death, and resurrection of Jesus.

It is important to note that one doesn't have to wait until the end of the sermon to engage in matters that fulfill the kerygmatic thrust. It has been said in many preaching circles that when you close, you have to go by the cross. However, the kerygmatic fulfillment offers the option to look at life, death, or resurrection as an interpretive expression of kerygma. This may come at the close of the sermon. However, it may also come in the midst of the sermon. Dr. Jones would call this kerygma in continuity. This simply means that the kerygmatic fulfillment may have been expressed in the course of the sermon, not just at the conclusion of the sermon. Moreover, this interpretive reality can be interpreted through the Old Testament or New Testament. In the words of Dr. Jones, "In the Old Testament, God gave us something. In the New Testament, God gave us someone." According to Dr. Jones, the Christian preacher's task isn't fulfilled until the bridge is built in the text to see the fulfillment of Jesus through either life, death, or resurrection.

The point of fulfillment of the sermon is to ensure that the preacher is fulfilling the purpose of the sermon, not just concluding the sermon. Using the organizing observation as a cornerstone/North Star, and the kerygmatic thrust as a guide will not only help us get to the indicative, but also the imperative of what must be done as a result of hearing the words of this sermon.

Let's look at an example of fulfilling the sermon on which we have been working. Below you will find the fulfillment. The sermon outline will be in the appendix.

ORGANIZING OBSERVATION

There are times when . . . *violence visits the vicinities in which we live.*
When such occurs . . . *this text teaches us how to proceed in partnership with God to gain victory over violence.*

Title: Victory Over Violence

FULFILLMENT

As we close this sermon, the scripture reminds us that if we want to have victory over violence, the text teaches us to have an attitude of reverence, engage in acts of resistance, so that one day we will be able to experience God's redemption. That's what these midwives did. And because of their reverence and resistance in Chapter 1, in Chapter 2 a child is born to a woman named Jochebed. Jochebed gave birth to a baby boy who had an edict issued against him to have him killed. And the child's name was Moses. Moses was born because two women dared to reverence God and act with resistance. And if you keep reading, you will see how Moses led his people out of slavery. Moses became a redeemer for his people. She gave birth to a boy who grew up to lead his people out of slavery. That's redemption. Because of what some midwives did, people gained victory over violence. But it didn't stop there.

Because if you keep on turning the pages, and if you keep walking the streets of the sacred text, you will find Joshua, son of Nun, and see how he took the reins after Moses, but don't stop there. Check out Deborah, and David. But don't stop there. Walk through the prophets and see how they called their countries into accountability. But keep on walking and make your way to a little small town in the south lands of Judah. And check out a child born to a poor teenage northeast African mother who reverenced and resisted. Born in a backyard barn in Bethlehem, born under a hater named Herod, who also issued an edict to have him killed.

But this little boy, who reverenced God. This little boy engaged in acts of resistance by confounding critics, turning over tables, and traveling with folks who would cut you in a heartbeat. He grew up in a culture of violence. This little boy grew up and went to a pool one day and healed the sick. He turned H_2O into merlot. In fact, the police record tells us that they beat him all night long and nailed him to some wood. But this victim of violence became a victor over violence. And because he lives, we can face tomorrow. Because he lives, we can have victory over violence.

In the closing of the sermon, you find fulfillment. The organizing observation with which we began was fulfilled by the sermon.

QUESTIONS TO CONSIDER

1. What does it mean to fulfill a sermon?
2. What is the difference between concluding and fulfilling a sermon?

NOTES

1. Martha Simmons, *Doing the Deed: The Mechanics of 21st Century Preaching* (Atlanta: The African American Pulpit, 2012), Location 2105 of 2650, Kindle Edition.

2. Ibid.

3. Frank A. Thomas, *They Like to Never Quit Praisin' God: The Role Of Celebration in Preaching* (Cleveland, OH: Pilgrim Press, 1997).

MOVEMENT

CHAPTER 8

IMPERATIVE

DON'T JUST TALK ABOUT IT, BE ABOUT IT

Earlier in the book, we engaged imagery for prophetic preaching, using the metaphor of prophetic preaching as an alarm. To recap, the sound of the alarm is expected to get people to move. In Chapter 3 of this book, we identified the indicative and imperative components of the kerygmatic fulfillment. It is the imperative component of kerygma that we now examine more fully, as we examine the expectation of the alarm on the movement of the masses.

Let us begin with a recap of the imperative.

IMPERATIVE

The imperative is the response to the indicative. Once the indicative is heard, there is some action that must take place as a result of hearing the indicative. The imperative is that which ought to be done, as a result of hearing the indicative. The imperative is about the lifestyle of transformation that comes as a result of hearing the indicative, which prayerfully serves as an impetus for transformation of not only the self, but society as well. In other words, what should be done as a result of hearing the indicative? What shall we do now, as a result of hearing what we have heard? What is the proclamation calling the people to be and do as a result of hearing the imperative?

The imperative is the response that is urged based on what is heard. What God has done in the indicative ought to have some impact on the imperative. That is, what God has done in the life, death, and resurrection of Jesus (indicative) ought to have some bearing on the response, which helps us to see what should be done now that we have heard the indicative. Put plainly, the imperative is about the movement as a result of the message. In the sermon explored in Part 2, the indicative helped us to see that we are called to have attitudes of reverence and acts of resistance in order to experience redemption. The sermon called on the people to do something as a result of something they heard. Prayerfully, this doing something will empower the people to change and/or engage in acts that bring change to society, which is the purpose of prophetic preaching.

In the article "How Do Sermons Help People Change?"[1] Ronald Allen undertook the task of discovering how sermons cause people to act or think differently. To do so, he polled 263 church attenders to ask them what was it about sermons that caused them to act or think differently. The dominant responses indicated that sermons that caused people to think or act differently did the following: (1) name the need for change, (2) a positive lure, (3) real stories as models of change, (4) seeing the world from other points of view, and (5) persons open to change when life is hard. Allen's assessment is helpful in ascertaining how people come to view sermons, and, more importantly, what people take from sermons.

Further, Allen is helpful in the announcement that one of the components that assists in people's transformation through sermonic presentation is the use of real stories as models of change. I assert afresh that sermons that engage the use of stories to help people to story themselves.

In my own investigation of the impact that sermons have on not only causing people to change, but causing people to engage in matters of justice, the results were a bit startling. In a study[2] investigating whether, among other things, sermons moved people to become active in matters of social justice, seventy members of a church were surveyed, 94 percent of respondents agreed (40 percent) or strongly agreed (54.29 percent) that it was important that sermons and Bible study inspired them to be active in matters of justice in church and community.

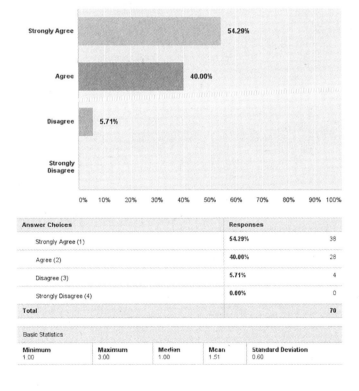

Answer Choices	Responses	
Strongly Agree (1)	54.29%	38
Agree (2)	40.00%	28
Disagree (3)	5.71%	4
Strongly Disagree (4)	0.00%	0
Total		70

Basic Statistics				
Minimum	Maximum	Median	Mean	Standard Deviation
1.00	3.00	1.00	1.51	0.60

Over 95 percent of respondents agreed (42.86 percent) or strongly agreed (52.86 percent) that authentic gospel preaching ought to address the political realities in the society in which we live.

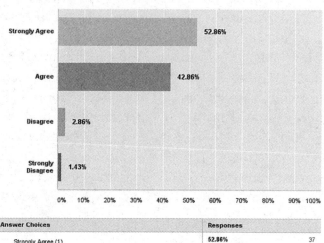

Answer Choices	Responses	
Strongly Agree (1)	52.86%	37
Agree (2)	42.86%	30
Disagree (3)	2.86%	2
Strongly Disagree (4)	1.43%	1
Total		70

Basic Statistics

Minimum	Maximum	Median	Mean	Standard Deviation
1.00	4.00	1.00	1.53	0.63

Over 95 percent of respondents stated that it was somewhat important (45.71 percent) or very important (50 percent) for the church to be involved in matters of politics.

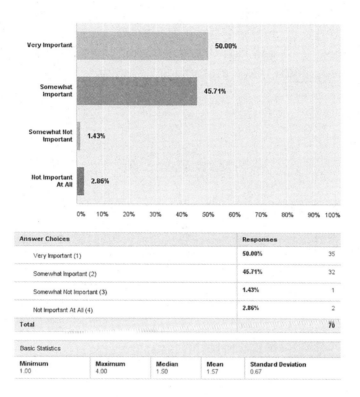

Answer Choices	Responses	
Very Important (1)	50.00%	35
Somewhat Important (2)	45.71%	32
Somewhat Not Important (3)	1.43%	1
Not Important At All (4)	2.86%	2
Total		70

Basic Statistics				
Minimum	Maximum	Median	Mean	Standard Deviation
1.00	4.00	1.50	1.57	0.67

In viewing the above responses, it would appear that the prevailing majority of respondents value and expect the church to be involved in matters of justice, political awareness, and education. This further indicates that these respondents expect the church to be prophetically involved in the work of community and justice-making. Moreover, they expect sermons, Bible study, and the work of the church to address and work toward a just society. These findings are affirming of my own expectations of church, preaching, and its witness in the world. Moreover, these results indicate that the majority of people in this context expect the church to be the place, among other things, that keeps tabs on what is going on, not only inside but also outside of the walls of the church.

Over 96 percent strongly agree (51.43 percent) or agree (45.71 percent) that the church should be involved in campaigns that lead to social change.

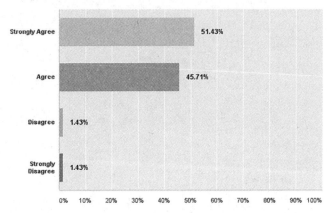

Answer Choices	Responses	
Strongly Agree (1)	51.43%	36
Agree (2)	45.71%	32
Disagree (3)	1.43%	1
Strongly Disagree (4)	1.43%	1
Total		70

Basic Statistics				
Minimum	Maximum	Median	Mean	Standard Deviation
1.00	4.00	1.00	1.53	0.60

Over 90 percent agree (52.86 percent) or strongly agree (38.57 percent) that they would personally get involved in a campaign that leads to social change.

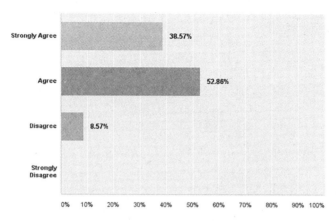

Answer Choices	Responses	
Strongly Agree (1)	38.57%	27
Agree (2)	52.86%	37
Disagree (3)	8.57%	6
Strongly Disagree (4)	0.00%	0
Total		70

Basic Statistics

Minimum	Maximum	Median	Mean	Standard Deviation
1.00	3.00	2.00	1.70	0.62

However, when asked about their actual personal involvement in any campaign to address any social justice issue within the past two years, almost 40 percent (37.14 percent) stated that they had not been involved in a campaign for any social justice issue in the past two years.

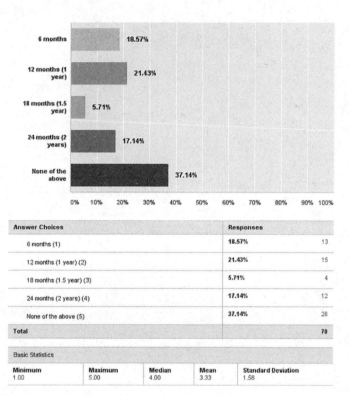

Answer Choices	Responses	
6 months (1)	18.57%	13
12 months (1 year) (2)	21.43%	15
18 months (1.5 year) (3)	5.71%	4
24 months (2 years) (4)	17.14%	12
None of the above (5)	37.14%	26
Total		70

Basic Statistics				
Minimum	Maximum	Median	Mean	Standard Deviation
1.00	5.00	4.00	3.33	1.58

This level of inaction is mind-blowing, given all of the social unrest and upheaval that occurred from 2014–2016, when this survey was taken. In that span of time, there were marches and efforts around police brutality and violence, boycotts of businesses in order to show the power of the Black dollar, campaigns against the decision to gut the Voting Rights Act, actions to support the passing of a budget in the state of Illinois, calls for government pressure to rescue the stolen girls of Chibok in Nigeria, efforts to cease child sex trafficking, and plenty of other opportunities to engage in action that leads to justice. Moreover, these matters were sermonically addressed and articulated with some organized actions from the pulpit of the church. Over 90 percent of people expect the church to do something, but almost 40 percent state that they have done nothing. To be fair, 17 percent stated they had been involved in some effort in the past two years, 5 percent said the past 18 months, 21 percent said the past year, and 18 percent said the past six months.

This gives rise to the following observations. One observation suggests that for some people, it is important to hear sermons engage in storying and for the church to be prophetically active and involved in the fight for justice. However, the difference in percentages between those who have actually acted and those who expect the church to act reveals the possibility that some expect the church to do the work and not them.[3] This observation gives an opportunity to investigate how some people understand church. Is it understood as an institution in which we are all to play a part and have responsibility, or is it an institution that, in a capitalistic consciousness, we pay to have activities done for us? Are we the church, or is the church a building to which we come for worship on Sundays? Is this an institution of them or us? Deeper still, do people understand the church to be those assigned to leadership? Are all members of the congregation and community seeking to walk in the way of love and liberation of Jesus the Christ? Again, the question must be asked: What do the people understand the church to be?[4] This question alone deserves deeper study.

Another observation suggests that almost 40 percent could be waiting on the church to provide the opportunity to engage in such action. Although some preaching, teaching, and actions from the church were organized, 40 percent of the people still confessed that they did nothing. This observation has awakened me to the fact that, while storying may be important, as well as preaching, both together are a very small part of leading the people into being the church that changes society. I overestimated the impact of preaching and storying in moving masses to doing the work of justice. While storying and preaching are important, and necessary in order to stand for justice, research has shown that both are also much less impactful in moving the needle for justice and change for people, policies, and politics than was previously perceived.

Therefore, when we speak of and identify moving the masses, we can no longer think of masses in terms of numbers, but as a critical mass. It is easy to think of masses as akin to numbers only, in a capitalistic context where we are taught to believe that the amount of people or products validates your preaching and/or your ministry. However, masses can be moved without a mass of people. While it is true that there is strength in numbers, it is also true that numbers are not the prerequisite for movement. Mega ministry can be done without being a megachurch. This is in no way meant to disparage those megachurches that are doing the work of prophetic mega ministry. There are many churches with large memberships preaching a prophetic gospel and engaging in prophetic ministry that meets the needs of masses. The number of persons to whom one preaches does not determine whether masses are being met and moved to change society for the better.

As you preach, explore your own context to consider the programs, policies, and people that will lead to the imperative of moving the masses for maximum impact regardless of numbers.

Here, we now highlight three prophetic preachers, whose ministries and messages exhibit what it means to move the masses. Each of them were asked how they understood the work of their preaching to connect with the movement of people in the work of prophetic ministry, justice, and righteousness.

REV. DR. MELVA SAMPSON

Melva L. Sampson is an assistant professor of preaching and practical theology at Wake Forest University School of Divinity. She is an ordained minister of the Progressive National Baptist Convention and an ordained ruling elder in the Presbyterian Church, USA. Her research interests live at the intersections of gender, digital interactive media, performance, and preaching. She is the creator and curator of Pink Robe Chronicles™, a digital hush harbor that centers faith and spirituality utilizing the womanist tenets of redemptive self-love, critical engagement, radical subjectivity, and traditional communalism to elucidate the role of sacred memory and ritual in the collective healing of marginalized communities.[5]

Dr. Sampson asserts that "authenticity is my superpower."[6] As such, she understands that the purpose of her preaching and teaching is to help people lean into uncovering and understanding their own authenticity. Dr. Sampson asserts this is important because in the midst of contexts of control expressed through "Western Culture, white body supremacy, capitalism, patriarchy, and the rest of the whole boat of oppressive and interlocking systems,"[7] people have to know who they are outside of these systems that have sought to define them. These layers have sought to disconnect, dehumanize, and denigrate people away from who they were created to be. Dr. Sampson connects her mandate, mission, and message to helping unlock who people are personally, and as a people. To do so, she employs four principles, which grounds her work, writings, and walk to help move the masses.

1. **Self Determination.** Sampson unpacks self-determination, or kujichagulia,[8] as beginning with seeing yourself as a subject and not an object as the dominant culture would have us to see ourselves. This is especially central to people's survival in a society that invites us, injects us, and injures us with images, and instances of attempts to reduce Black and brown bodies to simple objects to be used, and not people to be appreciated and loved. Self-determination means that the self must do this, not society. This understanding takes us back to the lenses through which we must look for prophetic preaching found in Chapter 2 of this book.

2. **Sankofa.** Sankofa means go back and fetch it, as demonstrated by the bird who looks back while positioning its body and feet forward. The role of Sampson's "digital hush harbor," the livestreams she calls Pink Robe Chronicles,™ is to create a space where people can go back and get the love for their flesh and have a place people "can go where Black enfleshment is

sacred."[9] In the days of chattel slavery in the United States, Africans would gather deep in the woods away from the eye of the overseer. In this space and place, enslaved Africans would gather in secret to experience the presence of the creator, and worship God in their own "cultural idiom and political space."[10] This is a "digital hush harbor that centers faith and spirituality using the womanist and Afrocentric values of self-determination, serious engagement, and liberating self-love to highlight the importance of collective work and responsibility in healing and sustaining marginalized communities."[11] In this digital hush harbor, safe space where the duality of sacred and secular is overcome, the whole of people is honored, thereby shifting how we've been socialized to see ourselves.

3. **Nommo.** Nommo is the creative word that suggests that once one speaks, it comes to pass. The power of your voice is so formidable that once you state the intended, it will occur. This is a countercultural, subversive stance for a people who have been taught that they were powerless and had tongues cut out of their mouths for speaking with power. This is an important underpinning in order to help people remember their power and the power in their voice.

4. **Ubuntu.** Ubuntu, which is roughly translated as, "I am because we are," embodies authenticity not so that I can just be authentic in my life, but because our superpowers are deeply connected. This is the linking of our lives.

Using these four strategies, Dr. Sampson understands herself to be a digital griot. The digital griot, especially in the times of virtual visitation during the COVID-19 pandemic reminds the people of their story. The griot is born into a tradition and trained in the culture, consciousness, and story of the people. The griot is called upon when the community is in crisis, to remind them of the authenticity of their story. This must be done in a space that is uninhibited by external oppressive contexts.

Dr. Sampson moves masses grounded in her four strategic principles that are key in her work as an African-centered womanist digital griot. Whether it's Sunday morning, or anytime throughout the week, Sampson from her own home, makes available the digital hush harbor that empowers masses to be moved.

REV. DR. EARLE FISHER

A native of Benton Harbor, Michigan, Earle J. Fisher graduated from Benton Harbor High School in 1996, earned an associate degree in liberal arts in 1999 from Lake Michigan College, a bachelor of science degree in computer science in 2003 from LeMoyne Owen College, and a master of divinity degree in May 2008 from Memphis Theological Seminary. As a dually ordained minister in the Christian Church (Disciples of Christ) and Missionary Baptist Church denominations, Fisher holds a PhD in the area of rhetoric, politics, and society. He serves as an adjunct instructor of contemporary theology at Rhodes College and senior pastor of Abyssinian Missionary Baptist Church in Memphis, Tennessee. Most of Fisher's academic work focuses on African American religious rhetoric, contemporary rhetorical theory, Black liberation theology, and the prophetic persona of Albert Cleage, Jr.[12] Fisher holds that his prophetic preaching connects with the movement of the masses through the intentional acknowledgment and articulation of the socio-political climate that affects the people to whom he is preaching, whether the people are in the pews or the virtual sanctuary.

His preaching is grounded in an understanding of liberation as emancipation plus empowerment. For Fisher, if we are only talking about emancipating people but not empowering people, then we are not dealing with all that is needed for liberating gospel. As he prepares his sermons, he is asking the question of how to move the masses in a way that not only speaks to the social and political realities but moves people into empowerment. Fisher, grounded in the understanding of empowerment, founded UPTheVote901, a grassroots organization created to increase voter turnout in every Memphis/Shelby County election and give more political power, information, and representation to people.

Fisher is steeped in an understanding of Jesus as one who moved masses as a radical revolutionary organizer of the poor and oppressed.[13] "We need to organize our people for political power—like Jesus did. This is what got him killed. Jesus was killed (executed by the state) because he had the audacity to inspire and organize oppressed people and convinced them that they possessed a divine power within them that the seal of the Roman government could not conquer."[14]

Fisher also holds that when it comes to moving the masses, we must understand that we are speaking in the immediate moment to a nonexistent physical audience.[15] This is so not just in a pandemic where we are speaking to people in the virtual sanctuary. But we are also speaking now in a way that serves to plant seeds for future masses yet unborn and/or unknown. In essence, we are building beyond our years to reach masses of which we know nothing of currently.

REV. DR. HEBER BROWN

Community organizer, social entrepreneur, base builder, and network weaver are all words that describe the work and expertise of Heber Brown, III, senior pastor of Pleasant Hope Baptist Church in Baltimore, Maryland.

For nearly two decades, Brown has been a catalyst for personal transformation and social change. He is the founding director of Orita's Cross Freedom School. Inspired by the Freedom Schools of the 1960s, Brown works to reconnect Black youth to their African heritage while providing them hands-on learning opportunities to spark their creative genius and build vocational skills. Additionally, in 2015, he launched the Black Church Food Security Network, a multi-state alliance of congregations working together to promote health, wealth, and power in the Black community. The BCFSN accomplishes this by partnering with historically African American churches to establish gardens on church-owned land and cultivates partnerships with African American farmers to create grassroots, community-led food systems.[16]

Brown understands the sermon as an extension of the work beyond the pulpit and the church. In no uncertain terms, he sees the sermon as an "organizing tool"[17] to move the masses. Every sentence and page has him thinking of the work and service that sentence and page has with respect to the desired end and purpose. Moreover, he is intentional about creating new and varied ways through his sermons and teaching to decolonize what we mean by this individualistic way of giving life to Christ. How do we give our lives to the way of Christ with this work so that singular ways of joining are not just personal but public?

As the founder of the Black Church Food Security Network, Brown is emboldened in his preaching, especially when a direct link is made between what he will be preaching for the 35 minutes in the pulpit and the work to be done for the next 30 hours of that week. Brown states, "If I know Friday I'm driving a 16-foot truck down to North Carolina to pick up produce, and I can connect this particular message with what I am about to do on Friday, then the proclamation becomes invitation—not just to walk down the aisle, but to get on the truck with me. Because now there is something I can invite you to that is more than just getting your name on the roll."

For Brown, moving the masses employs the sermon as an organizing tool.

CONCLUSION

This chapter has reviewed the importance of the work of the sermon. The imperative invites individuals to do something after having heard something. When we speak of moving the masses, we must take care not to reduce the definition of masses to numbers only. When we speak of masses, it's helpful to think of that term as critical masses. Sampson, Fisher, and Brown are flesh and blood examples of prophetic preachers who move masses through their work by starting where they are with what they have. They also remind us that moving the masses is more about impact than numbers!

NOTES

1. Ronald J. Allen, "How Do Sermons Help People Change," *Encounter* 69.1, 2008.

2. Reginald Williams, Jr. Phone Interview for *Moving the Masses: The Role of Prophetic Preaching in the Formation of a Prophetic Congregation,* Virginia Union University, Unpublished Doctoral Project Document for Doctor of Ministry, 2017.

3. This brings to bear another concern of how people visualize the church, and if they visualize themselves as the church. This could actually be the impetus for another study on the view of the church.

4. This question of who people understand the church to be also begs for further study. It would be interesting to ascertain this question with comparisons based on ethnic background, history, and heritage, status and class, and clergy v. non-clergy.

5. See https://www.drmelvasampson.com/about.

6. Interview with Dr. Melva Sampson on January 17, 2021.

7. Ibid.

8. Kujichagulia is one of seven principles of the Nguzo Saba. It means self-determination.

9. Interview with Dr. Melva Sampson on January 17, 2021.

10. Dwight Hopkins, *Shoes That Fit Our Feet* (Maryknoll, NY: Orbis Books, 1993), 18.

11. See https://www.drmelvasampson.com/pink-robe-chronicles, accessed April 23, 2021.

12. See https://www.memphis.edu/communication/people/grad_students/fisher.php, accessed April 28, 2021.

13. See http://www.stlamerican.com/news/local_news/rev-earle-j-fisher-calls-black-faith-community-to-political-action/article_3f3cb386-1c42-11ea-be2d-93d293c15934.html, accessed January 19, 2021.

14. Ibid.

15. Interview with Earle Fisher on January 17, 2021.

16. See https://www.heberbrown.com/about, accessed April 28, 2021.

17. Interview with Heber Brown on January 17, 2021.

CHAPTER 9

ACTION

*Preaching is the thermostat, which creates
the climate and atmosphere for
prophetic ministry to occur.*[1]
—REV. DR. FREDERICK DOUGLASS HAYNES, III

I'm blessed with two beautiful daughters who have caught the entrepreneurial bug. My youngest daughter, Laila, is the principal and founder of Laila's Lovely Creations. She makes bracelets and designs nails. My oldest is the principal and founder of Nia's Sweet Treats. She is an excellent baker of cakes, pies, and other delectable treats. Their respective pursuits make space for them to exhibit their awesome and amazing creativity.

With regard to Nia's Sweet Treats, the first thing Nia does is to turn on the oven to set the proper temperature for baking. Prior to and subsequent to the actual act of baking, Nia must engage in significant labor in order to ensure that the taste of the treat is full, flavorful, and fulfilling to her clients. Batter must be mixed, icing must be made, boxes to hold the finished product must be constructed, dishes must be washed, and a host of other responsibilities must be completed on either side of the mixed batter entering the oven. It is the oven, however, that is the instrument that sets the atmosphere for Nia's Sweet Treats to be cooked and completed.

Prophetic preaching serves as an oven of sorts. Prophetic preaching doesn't mix the dish, but sets the environment for the dish to be baked. Prophetic preaching sets the atmosphere for the work of liberation and transformation. Preaching does not do the work; it sets the stage, normalizes the temperature, and enlivens the atmosphere for movement work to be done after the preaching moment.

As an example, if a sermon is preached on voting, then some opportunities to learn about voting should be made available to those listening. If the sermon is about violence, then some resources that help to counter violence in our communities should be made available to the hearer. If a sermon is preached on financial stewardship and accountability, resources should be made available to support those looking to better themselves in this area. In this way, the preaching becomes the "earthy enterprise," in the words of Dr. Jones. We cannot just approach it by talking about it. The soil needs to be worked. For Dr. Jones, movement is the product of preaching, be it personally or publicly. He means movement, not in the sense of hollering and shouting, although that is cathartic, but when the sermon is done, and after the shouting and hollering, how has this sermon moved me to move toward an alternative reality? What must we do to be saved? The preaching does not just meet you in the moment but empowers the hearer to move toward a larger alternative reality.

CHARITY VS. JUSTICE

Prophetic preaching should be supported by, and lead to the creation of programs, policies, and practices which empower people to live into God-desired alternatives. In this creation of programs, ministries, and advocacy opportunities, it is important for the preacher to be able to name and articulate the difference between charity and justice. As stated in my previous book, co-authored with Rev. Danielle Ayers, *To Serve This Present Age*,[2] charity as defined, gives a sense of generosity and benevolence to a soul in need. In his book that offers stories of churches that move beyond charity toward justice, Niles Harper states: "Charity is understood to be works of love, acts of mutual aid, the duty of Christians . . ." This perspective emphasizes personal deeds of mercy and acts of compassion within the local community. Charity essentially becomes a reaction to something that has been done or is lacking in the life of another. Charity is essential but not exhaustive.

However, when we look at justice, it gives a different connotation altogether. Justice seeks to impartially maintain a system of equality, and right treatment. Unlike charity, justice is not reactive. Justice seeks the right relationships and right action from the inception. "Social justice focuses on basic causes of oppression, inequity, and disenfranchisement. It seeks to change public policy and public priorities. It works to empower people to take initiatives in ways that are positive and constructive. The movement for social justice understands that oppressed people have strengths, skills, cultural assets, and the responsibility to act corporately for their own common good." Whereas charity is reactive, justice is proactive.

Simply put, charity is meeting the need of a person or people in need. Justice is seeking to eliminate the need in the first place. In the example of a soup kitchen, charity is being offered by the soup kitchen. Hungry souls are being fed. Stomachs twisted and knotted by hunger pangs need to be fed. Therefore, as an act of charity, soup kitchens help to feed those who are hungry. However, the justice issue in this instance asks why is anyone hungry in the wealthiest country in the world? This hunger issue interfaces and interlocks with many other justice issues such as poverty and redistribution of wealth in a country hellbent on capitalistic manipulation in favor of the privileged.

Perhaps another illustration will help to clarify the difference between charity and justice. This illustration is often used from the pulpit and has even been seen as the mission statement for a church. There is a difference between a thermostat and a thermometer. The thermometer changes and reacts based on the environmental changes surrounding the thermometer. However, a thermostat changes the temperature of the environment surrounding it. The thermostat, like charity, reacts to what is going on around it. Charity reacts. The more the economy shifts downward, the more soup kitchens will open because there will be more homeless and more jobless people. However, while charity reacts to its environment, justice, like a thermostat, changes the environment. Justice is proactive. Justice seeks to eliminate the need for soup kitchens in the first place. Justice work—like a thermostat—places pressure on politicians and policy makers to ensure that none of God's children are too hot from the heat of oppressive measures or too cold from the wintry fingers of political and societal rejection. Justice work seeks to impartially balance the temperature and not just react to the temperature.

Archbishop Dom Helder Camara brings both of these separate yet related themes to bear when he says, "When I give food to the poor, they call me a saint. When I ask why they are poor, they call me a Communist." The archbishop's concern is still valid to this day. Oppressors are comfortable with charitable organizations and individuals. However, when systems that make charity necessary are challenged, problems arise. Challenging the systems through the work of justice will challenge the privilege and power of those who don't mind throwing a few crumbs of charity, but refuse to establish systems of equality, mutuality, reciprocity, and impartiality.

As such, we must remember that both charity and justice are essential to the work we do. The truth of the matter is that sometimes the focus on charity only impedes progress toward justice. Charity can cause people to accept things as they are, and never seek the change that justice provides so that charity will not be necessary. However, until the day comes where charity is not necessary, there must be an interlocked concerted effort that includes charity and justice! We do not have the luxury of forsaking justice for charity or charity for justice. We must employ both charity and justice in order to bring about a world where God's people will be treated as God would have them to be treated.

CONCLUSION

Prophetic Preaching is at once, an alarm and an oven. As stated earlier, it is an alarm, connected to the central surveillance system, intended to arrest our attention and announce that help is on the way. Prophetic Preaching is also an oven that sets the atmosphere for an alternative reality to come into existence. In order for God-desired alternatives to be realized, prophetic preaching must be in partnership with people, programs, communities, and others committed to the prophetic work of liberation and transformation. Prophetic Preaching does not do the work but sets the environment for the work to be done.

Moving the masses does not necessarily mean, moving the majority. History is a witness to the fact that the movements that have shaken up the world are the movements with a remnant. It's not about numbers. It's about impact! Revisionist historians would have us believe that the majority of people marched with Martin Luther King, Jr. This could not be further from the truth. It was a remnant of people who heeded his message from Montgomery to Memphis. In fact, Rev. Amos Brown, one of King's associate's is known to have said that in any given city, only 3 percent of African Americans were welcoming of King. Many thought he was a troublemaker, even when the trouble he came to make was for their progress. It ought not to be taken lightly, that while King was the voice, if it had not been for women who organized like Ella Baker, whatever movement that happened would have fallen flat on its face. For it was Ella Baker who said, "Give people the light and they will find the way."

Beginning with the unrest following the non-conviction of the murderers of Trayvon Martin, Alicia Garza, Opal Tometti, and Patrisse Cullors began a movement that lasts to this day. It has been a remnant of those in the movement for Black lives who have disrupted and interrupted business as usual to declare to this nation that Black Lives Matter.

It was a remnant of followers of the way of Jesus who began a movement that continues to transform lives to this day. As has already been stated, I am not talking about the Jesus crafted in the cauldron of white body supremacy, in the words of Resmaa Menakem.[3] I am talking about the Jesus who was a revolutionary Palestinian Jew, whose land was occupied by a Roman government, who ultimately was lynched due to his revolutionary deeds on behalf of the people, who threatened the agenda of the privileged, some of whom were his own people!

Prophetic preaching that moves the masses may not move the majority. I dare say, however, that prophetic preaching that moves from the internal storying to sermonizing will set the temperature for a remnant to change the world!

Prophetic preaching is born from an internal reckoning of one's soul and social location in the context of community, resulting in the announcement of God-desired alternatives to systems and ways of being affecting God's creation can empower the movement of masses to change the world.

May those who accept this responsibility of prophetic preaching serve as alarms to arrest people's attention and announce that help is on the way. May those who accept also serve as ovens to set the atmosphere for the work of transformation and liberation to be done.

With countercultural consciousness, courage, and care, may we all commit to the God-desired alternatives that announce and initiate authentic freedom and justice for all!

NOTES

1. Interview with Frederick D. Haynes III, on August 24, 2016.
2. Danielle Ayers and Reginald W. Williams Jr., *To Serve This Present Age* (Valley Forge, PA: Judson Press, 2013).
3. Resmaa Menakem, *My Grandmothers Hands: Racialized Trauma and the Pathway to Mending Our Hearts and Bodies* (Las Vegas: Central Recovery Press, 2017)

AFTERWORD

Arduously wrestling with word selection, employing perfect literary devices, and crafting every movement, while fighting the angst of not being heard, a person emerges at the sacred desk humbly presenting their offering in the form of preaching. Never content with the *call and response* emblematic of the Black preaching moment and finding little satisfaction in the shouts of "say it!" which typically alert the preacher that something special is happening, for Reginald Wade Williams Jr., prophetic joy emerges when the preached word becomes the catalyst for embodied transformation wherein listeners accept the divine double dare to strategically snatch freedom from the jaws of injustice. In *Moving the Masses*, Dr. Williams creates a homiletic process that merges sermon preparation with preacher authenticity, purposefully carving out sacred space where Spirit invites each hearer to the radical act of "doing the work their souls must have."

Before Dr. Williams masterfully crafted this process, and before the first word was typed, this book found its beginnings in a mother knowing that her son was called to be a force for substantive social change. Like the biblical Hannah, Marcelle Williams started Reginald on a trajectory that metaphorically delivered him into the homiletical arms of Jeremiah A. Wright Jr., baptized him in the refining presence of Miles Jerome Jones, and resurrected the rhythm of his soul on the ethical dance floor of Katie Geneva Cannon.

As a Doctor of Ministry student at the Proctor School of Theology, Reginald brought all these potent preparations to bear, with hopes of creating a definitive work that would equip preachers to move congregations from the complacency endemic of an anemic theology to the frontline of community-based social transformation fueled by unearthing the prophetic nature of the gospel. His efforts were frustrated until he took seriously the requirement to unearth his own authentic being, listen for the "sound of the genuine," and quiet self-deprecating cacophonies. In doing the difficult work, Dr. Williams found a man extensively gifted, beautiful to the core, and courageous enough to allow Spirit to see and heal his scars. And from that, this invaluable resource, *Moving the Masses*, was born.

Alison P. Gise Johnson, PhD
Associate Professor of Historical and
Theological Studies
Proctor School of Theology
&
"Reginald's Favorite Professor"

EPILOGUE

Be the matter what it may,
Always speak the truth;
Whether at your work or play,
Always speak the truth.
Never from this rule depart,
Grave it deeply on your heart,
Written 'tis upon your chart:
"Always speak the truth."
—ALFRED ARTHUR GRALEY

As a girl, our mother would sit at the bedside of her great-grandmother, Nancy Thompson, soaking in her wisdom. A double amputee, our great-great-grandmother could not physically walk through the world with our mother and her sisters to teach and show them how to be courageous Black women in a corrupted social order. She did, however, offer wisdom in words drawn from her hard-won knowledge of this cold world. One gift she gave them was this poem, "Always Speak the Truth." This poem became an heirloom in our family. She taught it to them. They taught it to us: me; my brother, Reggie; our sister, Joy; and our cousins. Nancy Thompson gifted to her progeny an ethic—a way of being with which our words should align, *always speak the truth.*

In *Moving the Masses*, my brother extends the ethic of our heirloom in his method for prophetic preaching. Counterintuitively, he posits prophetic preaching first as a contemplative practice. Prophetic *listening* is a prerequisite for prophetic preaching. This involves attention and intention to locate and unveil the True Self, while wrestling with the resonances between sacred literature and social life. Prophetic preaching first calls for an inward journey that precedes any sacred rhetoric worth its salt.

Our parents met as student organizers on an anti-hunger campaign in downstate Illinois with Operation Breadbasket, which later evolved into Operation PUSH, led by Rev. Jesse Louis Jackson. As children, we were at the PUSH headquarters on Saturdays almost as often as we were in church on Sundays. On Saturday mornings, we listened to calls from the PUSH "pulpit" for justice, dignity, and equity from preachers, politicians, labor organizers, and freedom fighters. "I AM Somebody!" Jesse would proclaim, leading us in a call-and-repeat liturgy. The following day we would sit in sanctuaries where most of the preachers we listened to limited their proclamation to personal piety and pastoral care. Very rarely, if at all, did the social concern of Saturday intersect with the preaching moment of Sunday morning.

However, sandwiched between Saturday and Sunday morning was Saturday night. Reggie and I would have our ears pressed to the speakers of our small boom box, listening to WBMX and WKKC, two of the first stations in Chicago to play rap on the radio. With our fingers on the record and play buttons and a blank tape loaded, we fancied ourselves low-tech deejays. We would sit for hours dubbing homemade mixtapes of Eric

B. & Rakim, Grandmaster Flash and the Furious Five, Whodini, Run DMC, and UTFO. On Saturday night, we found ourselves fascinated with a form of prophetic and poetic proclamation that integrated poetic lyricism, social analysis, and critical theological reflection. These emcees taught us the power of cadence, tone, syntax, wordplay, metaphor, and imagery. We listened to and learned every line we recorded.

> *A child is born, with no state of mind*
> *Blind to the ways of mankind*
> *God is smilin' on you, but he's frownin' too*
> *Because only God knows, what you'll go through*
> *You'll grow in the ghetto, livin' second rate*
> *And your eyes will sing a song of deep hate*
> *The place, that you play and where you stay*
> *Looks like one great big alley way.*
> — MELLE MEL, "THE MESSAGE"

It wasn't until our family joined Trinity United Church of Christ, under the leadership of Rev. Dr. Jeremiah A. Wright Jr., that we consistently heard prophetic preaching that integrated lyrical artistry, theological reckoning with social evil, and visions of Black liberation. We were privileged to sit and soak that in Sunday after Sunday for much of our later adolescence and young adulthood. There is no substitute for listening to the sound of masterful preaching.

In December 1997, at the age of 48, our mother took flight to rest with the ancestors. Nearly two years later, with broken hearts still saturated in grief, Reggie and I both entered seminary, Reggie at the School of Theology at Virginia Union University and me at the

Interdenominational Theological Center in Atlanta. Suffering has a strange way of inviting us to listen to our inner lives. Parker Palmer observes that there are two ways the heart can break. Hearts can shatter, leaving scattered shards unable to hold anything beyond their own weight. Hearts can also be broken open, a strange enlargement of the heart's capacity to hear and bear an expanded range of human emotion, suffering, and joy. You never know in the moment which way the break will occur. For Reggie and me, this heartbreaking loss and grief generated deep dissatisfaction with performative religion that fails to take suffering seriously.

At Virginia Union, my brother's exploration of the art and science of prophetic preaching began to take shape under the tutelage of Rev. Dr. Miles Jerome Jones. Dr. Jones insisted on authenticity as the ground from which prophetic preaching emerges. He accompanied Reggie into the unveiling of his True Self as he dug deeper into the wells of the prophetic homiletical tradition. Dr. Jones helped facilitate a path toward Reggie's reckoning with his inner life as a route to connection with the common condition of our people. That fundamental connection to authentic selfhood, through which we access our shared humanity, enables us to imagine alternative ways of being together in community.

This book is born of a life of listening—to inherited wisdom, to the language of liberation, to homiletical ingenuity, to the lyrical wizardry of hip-hop, to the disillusioning insights of suffering, and ultimately to the invitation of the inner teacher. I'm grateful to bear witness to this listening life, even as it continues to unfold. The method offered in *Moving the Masses* is born of a way of being with which Reggie's written words align. May this method invite the prophetic preacher to embody our great-great grandmother's ancestral ethic, *Always speak the truth.*

Matthew Wesley Williams
President of the Interdenominational Theological
Center
Atlanta, GA

APPENDIX A

CORRELATION METHOD SERMON OUTLINE WORKSHEET

- Title
- Organizing Observation
  - There are times when . . .
  - When such occurs . . .
- Introduction
- RQ/Transition into Text
- Moves or Points (answer the invitation / question)
  1. Points / Move 1
     a. Image
     b. Explanation
     c. Illustration
     d. Application
  2. Point / Move 2
     a. Image
     b. Explanation
     c. Illustration
     d. Application
  3. Point / Move 3
     a. Image
     b. Explanation
     c. Illustration
     d. Application
- Kerygmatic Fulfillment

APPENDIX B

CORRELATION METHOD SERMON GRADING SHEET

PROPHETIC PREACHING

CORRELATION METHOD

Name of Preacher:

Scripture Text (2.5%):

Organizing Observation of the Sermon (40%):

TAT

WSO

Title (2.5%):

Introduction (10%):

Transition / Relevant Question (15%):

What Moves / Points of Progression Did You Note (10%):

Kerygma (10%):

Hallmarks of Prophetic Preaching (10%):

General Notes:

APPENDIX C

POINT DEVELOPMENT

IMAGE
Paint the picture of the text as it relates to this point
List the five senses

EXPLANATION
Explain any historical/exegetical relevance

ILLUSTRATION
Applicable story or run to emphasize the point

APPLICATION
How does this emphasis of the point apply to the people?

APPENDIX D

SAMPLE CORRELATION
SERMON OUTLINE
(VICTORY OVER VIOLENCE)

Method of Preaching
Exodus 1:15-22
Sermon Outline Example

ORGANIZING OBSERVATION

There are times when . . . *violence visits the vicinities in which we live.*
When such occurs . . . *this text shows us how to proceed in partnership with God to gain victory over violence.*

Title: Victory Over Violence
Intro: In 1971, Marvin Gaye wrote a song that was part of an album with the same title. And in that song, he asked a very important question. When he looked around and saw how war was killing innocent people. When he looked around and saw how racism was violating his own people. When he saw how people could fight for their country, then come home and be treated like trash by the same country they fought for, Marvin asked this question, "What's Going On?" Marvin asked a question in order to gain some understanding, because he realized that there are times when violence is the unwelcome visitor that visits the vulnerable. We know something about that right here in Chicago, don't we? When we look and see how it is easier to get a gun than it is a loaf of bread in a food desert, we can attest to the

fact that violence visits our vicinities. When such occurs, however, the text shows us that we can partner with God to gain victory over violence.

TRANSITION
Transition: *Come with me, and let's see how the text shows us how we can gain victory over violence.*

or

RQ: *Well, the question is: How can we gain victory over violence?*

MOVES/POINTS:

- Attitude of Reverence (v. 17a)
  - Image—Can you see the midwives? Paint the picture of midwives being called into the office and told that they have to kill babies, which they knew God would not have them to do.
  - Explanation—Explain the meaning of the word "feared." The word for feared in this text does not mean scared of, but in awe of. They reverenced God because they had a relationship with God. And they knew that God would not have them kill any child.
  - Illustration—Use the story of the pastor whose reverence for God caused him to make a hard decision.
  - Application—Application of reverence. When you reverence God, you won't just take someone's life. You won't just kill, either through a gun or through policies.

- Acts of Resistance (v. 17b)
  - Image—Give the image of the midwives resolving to resist. They are told to do one thing, but they resist and do what God told them to do! Paint the picture of what they were thinking, and possibly what they were saying.
  - Explanation—They could be killed for denying the order of the Pharaoh. But they dared put their life on the line in order to resist.
  - Illustration—Story about resistance.
    - Bully beating up a boy. Momma tells him that you will fight back or you will deal with me.
    - Call the role of people who resist.
  - Application
    - How do we resist? How does the illustration help us to see how to resist? What are some ways that we can use the midwives, models to engage in resistance in our lives?
- Acceptance of Redemption
  - Image—(v. 20) So God dealt with the midwives, and the people multiplied and became very strong.
  - Explanation—Explain what redemption means, and how it is seen in the text. It means that the people were saved and preserved from what could have happened. Children grew up and were given a chance at life because some people made the decision to reverence God and resist government.
  - Illustration—Lift up stories of people who were saved because someone dared engage in some kind of resistance.

- Application—Help people see how others' reverence and resistance has helped our people be redeemed or saved.

KERYGMATIC FULFILLMENT

These women were resisting because they feared God could be seen as a means for Moses to be born. Moses led his people to liberation. Who knows what child you may let live, leading to a people's liberation? Because I know someone else who was born in the midst of an edict that wanted all the children killed. I know someone else who was born but had some people who listened to the Lord and hid him to protect him. (LIFE)

Or

I know someone else, who engaged in reverence, and resistance. He was often in prayer. And he knew how to resist. He turned over the tables in the temple. And we are redeemed because of his reverence and resistance. And because he lives, I can face tomorrow.

IMPERATIVE

So let us leave this place with the model of the midwives.

- So as we leave this place, let us leave being more resolved to engage in proper *reverence* for our God.
- Let us be committed to *resisting* any policies of the Empire that:
  - Take human life
  - Violates the vulnerable
- So that we may be in partnership with God in the *redemption* of our people.